W9-BDS-992

BATTLE TALK!

BEST WISHES TO

BILL STUDER,

Dick Hill

BATTLE TALK!

MEMOIRS OF A MARINE RADIO CORRESPONDENT

DICK HILL

Beaver's Pond Press, Inc.

Edina, Minnesota

BATTLE TALK!: MEMOIRS OF A MARINE RADIO CORRESPONDENT © copyright 2006 by Dick Hill. All rights reserved. No part of this book may be reproduced in any form whatsoever, by photography or xerography or by any other means, by broadcast or transmission, by translation into any kind of language, nor by recording electronically or otherwise, without permission in writing from the author, except by a reviewer, who may quote brief passages in critical articles or reviews.

ISBN 10: 1-59298-155-0
ISBN 13: 978-1-59298-155-7

Library of Congress Control Number: 2006905470
Printed in the United States of America
First Printing: August 2006
10   09   08   07   06   6   5   4   3   2   1

Cover and interior design by Clay Schotzko

Beaver's Pond Press, Inc.

Beaver's Pond Press, Inc.
7104 Ohms Lane, Suite 216
Edina, MN 55439-2129
(952) 829-8818
www.BeaversPondPress.com

To order, visit www.BookHouseFulfillment.com or call 1-800-901-3480. Reseller discounts available.

DEDICATION

This book is dedicated to the United States Marine Corps Combat Correspondents Association. The USMCCCA comprises former Marines, active-duty and retired Marine journalists, photographers, authors, artists, motion picture, radio-television broadcasters, and related professionals. These courageous Marines dedicate their lives and careers to informing the American public about the Marine Corps and its programs, activities, and achievements. Over 40 CCs lost their lives in combat in World War II, the Korean War, Viet Nam, and subsequent actions. I am deeply proud to say it is the only organization of its kind in the U.S. military services.

For more information on Combat Correspondents, go to the web: *www.usmccca.org*

CONTENTS

PREFACE

If not for the keen eyes of Mary Hill, my wife, this book probably would not exist. Cleaning the basement, she saw my duffel bag from the Marines. Inside she discovered radio tapes, journals, photos, and documents from my Korean War duty in 1952–1953. For nearly 50 years, the material was "lost." The Marine Corps Public Affairs office in New York, hearing about the find, called it a historical gold mine. The duffel bag of tapes and memories resulted in *Battle Talk! Memoirs of a Marine Radio Correspondent.*

This is my memoir and battlefield report. It is the only book to use transcripts from actual radio reports, including an interview with baseball Hall of Famer, Ted Williams. This is also the only book to address the special bond between the media and the Marines. And the only book to touch on the media circus atmosphere at the Public Information Office (PIO) news tent.

I was a young announcer at a small-town radio station when I answered my call of duty. I switched microphones and became a Marine Radio Correspondent. After boot camp and weeks of intensive combat training, I was assigned to PIO, now called Public Affairs. I was part of the finest public relations team in the military, Marine Combat Correspondents.

Combat Correspondents are the Marine Corps' news reporters. They are the bold, skilled professional writers, photographers, cameramen, broadcast reporters, artists, and others who keep the public informed about Marine Corps activities. They follow their fellow Marines all over the world. They train side-by-side with the warfighting units. As part of the Public Affairs section, they are the link between the Marines and the American public. To accomplish their mission, the CCs must have a sound understanding of the Marine Corps' organization and tactics used in war and other conflicts.

Long before today's high-tech communications, it was just pens and pads. That was in the beginning in 1775 when the U.S. Marine Corps was established by the Continental Congress. Thomas Jefferson and our Founding Fathers needed more firepower to fight the Revolutionary War. One of the troops, usually the guy with the best nose for news, was designated as a reporter. At the end of each day, after soldiering with his fellow Marines, he jotted down what he saw. It sometimes took weeks for news reports to reach the public. Today the flow of information is instantaneous.

Battle Talk! is a landmark book for fans of history, the media, or war stories. You will get as close to Marine Boot Camps as anyone, without enlisting. You will hear about Sgt. Francis Grunert's brief captivity as a prisoner of war (POW) held by the Chinese. Sports fans will read about Marine Corps athletes and hear about Ted Williams' close call with a jet. Travel buffs will learn about Asian rest-and-relation (R&R) holidays. And of course you will read battlefield reports. If you admire the achievements of the Marine Corps, then you'll also admire *Battle Talk!*

Thanks to the miracle of 3M audio tape, my radio reports of America's Forgotten War are now "replayed" by way of transcripts and memoirs. And thanks to digital audio technology, you'll be able to hear the actual voices and sounds from the Korean War, now on a CD, inside the back cover. Enjoy. *Semper Fi*, readers.

ACKNOWLEDGEMENTS

Marines are quick to help each other. I am indebted to many fellow combat correspondents, and others, for their helping hand and words of encouragement. A special salute to all those involved, including:

Lee Ballenger

William Bierd

Stan Bird

James Brady

Frank Burke

John Chalk

William Daum

David Douglas Duncan

Walt Ford

Don Gee

Francis Grunert

Joe Hensley

William Hopkins

Bob Johnson

Frank Kerr

Raymond Maurstad

Jack Paxton

Frank Praytor

John Rash

Leonard "Shifty" Shifflette

Associations and Organizations

A/1/7 Marine Corps Association - Korea: 1950–1953

Associated Press

Chosin Few Association - Korea 1950

Doubleday, Division of Random House, Inc.

Leatherneck magazine

Minnesota Historical Society

National Archives

Public Affairs, United States Marine Corps

Harry Ransom Humanities Research Center

United States Marine Corps Combat Correspondents Association

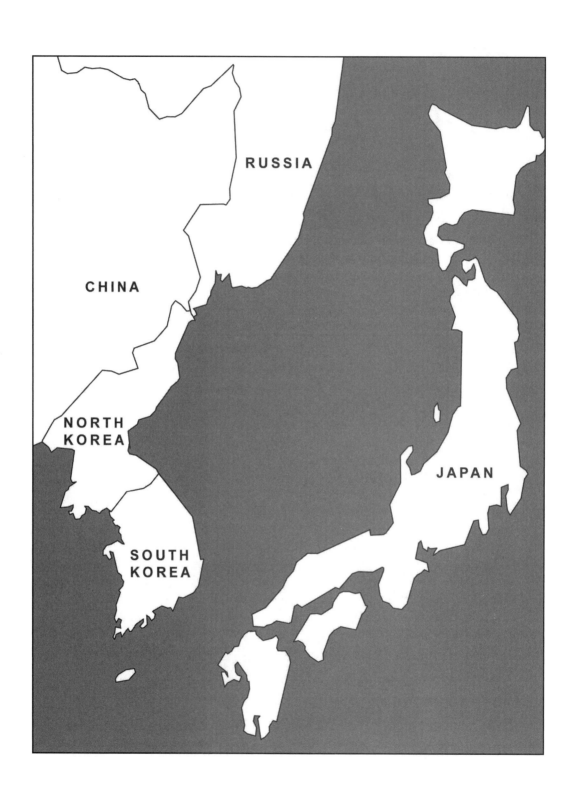

1

WHERE'S KOREA?

Small-town radio stations offer great training for wannabe announcers. I was young, eager, and learning my trade at WBIZ in Eau Claire, Wisconsin. Population: 25,000. WBIZ was 1330 on the dial, broadcasting on a feeble signal of 250 watts. In radio, you wear lots of hats. I was an announcer, disc jockey, newsman, sportscaster and part-time salesman of advertising time. Also, I had to check the program log for the next commercial, keep one eye on our United Press (UP) wire service for breaking news, answer the phone, and sound "cool" when on the air. On top of this, Jerry Thomas, our morning announcer and my evening sidekick, interrupted my concentration. Jerry was checking the UP news machine for me just as I was introducing Rosemary Clooney's newest hit tune, "Tenderly." He shouted from the news room, "Hey, Dick!"

It was June 25, 1950. "Where's Korea?" Jerry shouted.

I was able to hit the off-button before anyone could hear him. "Why do you want know?" I hollered back.

"It's on the wire. Some breaking news. It looks like war. The Communist North Koreans just invaded South Korea."

Where's Korea? Most Americans did not know that Korea sits just below Manchuria, in the eastern part of China. The early reports from our UP news service were sketchy. Communist North Korean soldiers were rushing past the 38th parallel into South Korea, headed for Seoul, the capital. The United Nations called it a violation of international peace. Little did I know at the time that I would soon be broadcasting from Korea. Oh, how war changes lifestyles, especially when you have to travel 6,350 miles to a spot in Asia that few people know about.

1

YELLOW LEGS

North Korean soldiers feared the "yellow leg men," the Marines, who wore yellow leggings.

While I was reporting the North Korean invasion on WBIZ, a fellow Minnesotan, Raymond Maurstad, a young Maritime radio officer, was in the thick of it. He was one of the handful of American advisors in Seoul. His book, *SOS Korea 1950*, tells about the utter chaos and confusion that resulted in South Korea following the attack. General Douglas MacArthur, in the Dai Ichi Building in Tokyo, was cut off for a time from communications with his officials in Korea. So Maurstad and some of his friends, using their own personal amateur radio equipment, kept MacArthur's headquarters informed about the deteriorating military situation. Soon after, the evacuation of 2,500 Americans from Seoul started. Mothers and their children were first to go. Transported from assembly points to Inchon, they were then placed aboard a fertilizer ship that was in port.

Maurstad's book tells about the last plane out of Seoul from Kimpo Airfield. The event also turned out to be the "first plane in" for war correspondents. Robert J. Rudolph, with the American Embassy, told about it in *SOS Korea 1950*:

> As the last C-54 aircraft arrived over Kimpo, we all waved white towels or T-shirts. I think we all felt rather foolish about doing so. The plane landed and taxied toward the air terminal while two P-51 Mustangs continued flying cover over us. I was enjoying the drama of the last plane's arrival. The C-54 swung into position in front of the terminal. The cargo doors opened to reveal two crewmen holding submachine guns with ammo clips in place. They looked out at us grimly. Here was a scene we could tell our grandchildren about. Then the crewmen put the ladder in place

and four civilians appeared in the plane's doorway. They were American reporters. Three of them were men. [Keyes Beech, *Chicago Daily News*, Frank Gibney, *Time*, Burton Crane, *New York Times*.] The fourth was a pretty young woman who looked fetching in a white blouse and dark skirt. She was Marguerite Higgins, a star reporter for the *New York Herald Tribune*.

NO SURPRISE

The media was better prepared for the Korean War than the U.S. Army. They —the reporters—hit the ground hours after the war started.

What a contrast. While most people were desperate to flee, some reporters were eager to arrive. Higgins was the first female reporter to witness America's entry into the battle for Korea. Maurstad said he met her and saw her as a "gutsy" lady. Sgt. Frank Kerr, a fellow Marine Combat Correspondent acting as a rifleman with the First Provisional Marine Brigade at the time, agreed that Marguerite Higgins was aggressive. Kerr, a gentleman, did not use the word "pushy." Yet I am sure she had to be demanding and blunt to get her stories written and dispatched in the war-torn country. There were limited communication lines in and out of Korea. Most had been cut or bombed. The few lines left were saved for the military's more urgent requests to the U.S. Army's headquarters in Japan.

Miss Marguerite Higgins made quite a name for herself with her early war reports from Korea. The next year (1951) her best selling book, *War in Korea, The Report of A Woman Combat Correspondent*, was published by Doubleday and Company. The photos, by *Life* photographer, Carl Mydans, and the U.S. Marine Corps, were worth the price alone.

It is no secret that many of the first U.S. Army troops sent into Korea from Japan were not combat ready. The Joint Chiefs of Staff had not favored the use of Ameri-

ORPHAN ARMY

Early in the war, Syngman Rhee smartly turned over his South Korean Army to MacArthur's command. Rhee's troops were no match for North Korea.

can ground forces in Korea, primarily because they knew how unprepared they were for large-scale combat. Yet MacArthur had to work with what he had at the moment. Also, South Korean President Syngman Rhee requested that America take over the Republic of Korea's Army leadership. Rhee knew his army was no match for the better trained and equipped North Korean troops. Here's a summary of Rhee's request, from Raymond Maurstad's book, *SOS Korea 1950*:

> Dear General MacArthur:
>
> In view of the common military effort of the United Nations on behalf of the Republic of Korea, in which all military forces, land, sea and air, of all the United Nations fighting in or near Korea have been placed under your command, I am happy to assign to you command authority over all land, sea and air forces of the Republic of Korea during the period of the continuation of the present state of hostilities, such command to be exercised either by you personally or by such military commander or commanders to whom you may delegate the exercise of this authority within Korea or in adjacent seas.
>
> The Korean Army will be proud to serve under your command.
>
> With continued highest and warmest feelings of personal regard,
>
> Sincerely yours,
>
> Syngman Rhee

General MacArthur confronted the United Nation's worst international crisis, and also had an orphan army that needed babysitting.

At home, U.S. military enlistments skyrocketed. After North Korea's invasion on June 25, young men headed to recruitment centers to do their part. One volunteer was Francis Grunert, 20, from Trenton, New Jersey, whom I was to meet and interview in the 7th Regiment's medical aid tent. He had seen John Wayne's newest war epic, *Sands of Iwo Jima*. That movie, plus the threat of war, convinced Grunert and others to join the Marines. On August 8, 1950 he enlisted and was rushed to Parris Island, South Carolina for basic training. Meanwhile, not as eager to serve in another war was Ted Williams, the Boston Red Sox hitting champion, whom I also interviewed. Playing his best baseball, he wasn't anxious to interrupt his career a second time. He didn't think there was a Chinaman's chance

Capt. Ted Williams updates poster after being activated into the Marines. Before going to Korea, he trained as a jet pilot at Cherry Point, North Carolina. (Marine Corps Photo)

they'd call him back in service. Besides, he was 32. Why would they want him? But the Marines needed jet pilots. So the Marines' most famous sports star got his papers. He reported at midnight, May 1, 1952 to Cherry Point, North Carolina, not far from where that young, eager Marine, Francis Grunert, took his boot camp. The two would never meet. But both would become Korean War heroes. (As featured in separate stories: *Ted Williams' Close Call* and *The Lucky Leatherneck*.)

While an announcer at WBIZ, Eau Claire, Wis., the author responded to the call of duty. He traded microphones, from reporting the Korean news as a civilian to reporting from the war front, as a reporter. (Photo Courtesy WBIZ Radio)

Thousands started filling the ranks that were needed in the war, myself included. And many of my friends from the reserves—Army, Navy, Air Force and Marines—were headed there also. I wasn't the only one that would be part of the United Nations forces—their first war since the UN's inception in 1945.

UN'S FIRST WAR

And mine, too. Most of my buddies were headed for Korea.

Americans soon knew where Korea was, and learned about its history. Scientists have evidence that people settled in what is now Korea, by at least 30,000 years ago. It was in 1895 when the Japanese gained control of Korea. They made it part of Japan in 1910. After the Allies defeated Japan in World War II (1939–1945), both United States and Soviet forces moved into Korea. It was a little bit like Germany after the war; Korea also was split in two. Soviet troops occupied Korea north of the 38th parallel of north latitude, an imaginary line that cuts the country about in half. I remembered some of this from attending Central High School in Minneapolis. American troops got the southern part of Korea (south of the 38th parallel). In 1947, the United Nations General Assembly tried to get the two Koreas together. They declared that elections should be held throughout Korea to choose one government for the entire country. The Soviet Union as much as said: "No way!" They alone opposed the idea and would not permit elections in their northern section of Korea. On May 10, 1948, the people of South Korea elected a national assembly. It set up the government of the Republic of Korea. On September 9, North Korean Communists established the Democratic People's Republic of Korea. Both North and South Korea claimed the entire country, and their troops clashed near the border sev-

7

South Korean family washing clothes at Imjin River. They appear oblivious to the war all around them. (Author's Collection)

eral times from 1948–1950. The United States removed its last troops from Korea in 1949 and announced early in 1950 that Korea laid outside the main U.S. defense line in Asia. This was the wrong message to send. The Communists believed the time was right for military action. Thus the invasion of South Korea on June 25, 1950, by the Communist North Koreans began.

No war is without its mistakes. The Korean War proved to be a nightmare and too much for the United Nations. (It was the first war in which a world organization played a military role.) Its commander in chief of the UN Command, General Douglas MacArthur, underestimated the potential force of the enemy. In the fall of 1950, after the successful Inchon landing by the Marines, MacArthur promised the troops they'd be home by Christmas. This assumption was based on North Korea's sole participation in the war. (They had 260,000 troops.) Then in November, masses of Communist Chinese soldiers joined in. Eventually, 780,000 more of the enemy troops were on the battle field—the world's biggest army. Good God! Can you imagine President Harry Truman's reaction when his Joint Chiefs of Staff told him this news? Heads would roll. (And they did.) And the worst part was that the Red Chinese were better trained and equipped than their counterparts, the North Koreans. The Red Chinese had been fighting Generalissimo Chiang Kai-shek's troops for years over the rightful ownership of China. They pushed the Nationalists off mainland China in 1949. The Nationalist leader, Chiang Kai-shek, declared Taipei, on the island of Taiwan, the capital of the Republic of China. Now, the Communist Chinese owned mainland China. They were warmed up and ready to take on the UN forces in Korea with the help of North Korea and Russia.

The war was fought from static positions during my tour in Korea, from 1952–1953. The Communist Chinese fought nose-to-nose with the Marines on the Main Line of Resistance (MLR.) They liked to "raise hell" with the Marines with both sniper and mortar fire, which I personally experienced while taping radio stories with our riflemen and others. We may have laughed at their meager uniforms—some of us called them pajamas—but we didn't laugh at their determination and warfare tactics. Nor did we laugh at their dirty tricks on our prisoners.

Today, everyone knows where Korea is. And it continues to be in the news. For all readers, including military history buffs and students of all ages, I only hope these pages add new interest and insight regarding America's Forgotten War.

IN THE NEWS - 1950

North Korea invades South Korea

Racial integration in U.S. Armed Forces

Blacklisting of Hollywood stars

A proud graduate and a PFC, the author and Platoon 391 at San Diego Marine Recruit Depot in January 1952. Author is in 2nd row, 7th from left, just above his boot camp DIs. (Marine Corps Photo)

2

THE BOOT FACTORY

My older brother, Kenny, who was in the Army during World War II, tried to tell me there was no difference between the Army's basic training and my Marine boot-camp training. As politely as I could, I told him if he believed that, then he probably believed there was no difference between the New York Yankees and my two grandsons' Little League Team. Which, by the way, was pretty good, but a few years away from playing with baseball's winningest team.

Boot camp is twelve weeks of Marine Corps hell. Recruits, forged in a furnace of tough training and shared hardship, become Marines. The Marine Corps' "boot factory" molds and transforms you into a steeled and confident Marine. At least that is what it seemed like to me. It was an adventure I will never forget.

It started in Minneapolis with a three-day train run to Los Angeles, then a short bus ride to the San Diego Marine Corps Recruit Depot. It was November of 1951 and the Korean War was heating up. From the news reports, the Marines and the United Nations forces needed us in a hurry.

Twenty of us from Minnesota, Iowa, North Dakota, South Dakota, and Wisconsin headed to Chicago to catch the train bound for Los Angeles. As we boarded, we joined maybe 30 other Marine recruits. The train was a beauty, operated by the Chicago and Northwestern Railway. I had seen it in movie newsreels. The car's interior featured newly invented materials of Formica and Naugahyde. Our train had a 50-seat diner car. It was the first time I had experienced train food and service. Great meals. Top notch service, too. We camped there a lot. Knowing where we were headed, the waiters sure took good care of us. A few times they treated us to free dessert. And with my six-dollars-a-day per-diem food allowance from

NICE WELCOME

Three DIs greeted us at the end of our train ride to LA. They escorted us to the San Diego boot camp. The Marine Corps now owned us.

the Marines, I was living high off the hog. On stops at St. Louis, Kansas City, and Denver, more recruits boarded the train. I talked with some. They were gung ho about the chance to fight in Korea. A few were only 17. I was 21.

During the trip we got to know each other pretty well, mostly through card games and shooting the breeze about sports and girls. When we kicked around the subject of boot camp, we agreed that the training might be too demanding for some. The Marine Corps did not tolerate underachievers. Heck, we knew that from watching John Wayne movies. One guy from Wisconsin said his brother had gone through "the boot factory" years before. We'd sure find out what he meant by that.

Finally, the City of Los Angeles train pulled to a stop in Los Angeles's busy Union Station. We were welcomed by 70-degree weather and three Marine greeters. Two were corporals. The one who seemed to be in charge wore three sergeant stripes. None wore smiles. The sergeant held a swagger stick and was wearing a trooper-campaign hat. The three Marines would have made good models for recruiting posters. They were alert, Hollywood-tanned and had the sharpest creases in their uniforms I had ever seen. Conversely, we were tired, wrinkled, and white as Minnesota snow. The three Drill Instructors (DIs) lined us up and sized us up. They were all business. With a war on I could understand their no-nonsense demeanor. They checked the roster, called roll, and herded us toward two just-washed Marine buses. The gravy-train ride was over. The Marine Corps now owned us.

The scenic drive from Los Angeles to San Diego was spoiled by the uncertainties of the road ahead. Korea we could take. Boot camp we wondered about. Some were scared as hell, and we were not even there yet. As a tall, good-looking Marine sentry at the gate gave the high sign for the buses to enter, I caught a glimpse of the beautiful training center with its lush green grass in the middle of November. And the Spanish architecture—reddish tile roofs on yellow stucco buildings—was something new for a Minnesota boy. Out on the parade grounds—about ten football fields big—hundreds of recruits were marching, marching, marching. Our turn was coming.

COMMON SENSE

Two rules I learned about weapons in boot camp could save the lives of hundreds of civilians. 1. Always consider your weapon loaded. 2. Never point it at anyone you do not intend to shoot.

They ordered us off the buses and marched us over to the mess hall for a late lunch. Somehow you felt out of step when you marched in civilian clothes, called "civvies." It was 3pm—that is, 1500 military time, as we learned our second day—and the stoves were shut down, so we were served cold ham and Swiss cheese on rye bread with a big scoop of potato salad. You could have as much cold milk as you wanted. It was our first Marine Corps chow. So far so good.

Platoon 391 was a mixed bag of recruits. There were 60 of us. In addition to our Midwest group, there were others from California, Illinois, Missouri, Puerto Rico, and Texas. Our platoon made history in 1951 because we were integrated. Before 1951, blacks and whites were segregated in the military. From then on it became regular practice to integrate African-Americans and whites. President Truman ordered it. (About time!) We were construction workers, truckers, farmers, ranchers, short-order cooks, clerks, students and one

TOP SONGS - 1950

"Be My Love"
        - Mario Lanza

"Mona Lisa"
        - Nat "King" Cole

"White Christmas"
        - Bing Crosby

radio announcer. We were all shapes and sizes, too. If you were overweight, boot camp would reshape you, pronto. While most of my peers lost excess fat, I filled out. I went from 125 pounds to 140.

Health and fitness have long been recognized as key to combat readiness. Marines use a progressive program of Physical Training (PT) to build up recruits to Marine Corps standards. The combination of physical exercise, balanced meals, and a 12-hour training schedule per day was a demanding regimen. PT included exercises, running, 10-mile conditioning marches, and obstacle courses.

Some of the younger guys in platoon 391 were surprised at all the classroom time in boot camp. Some thought they were getting away from school. They just wanted to rush into combat in Korea. One of the big reasons for the success of the Marine Corps is its emphasis on schooling and continuing education. Academic training exercised our minds and prepared us for battle. We studied Marine Corps traditions and history, general orders, combat principles, map-and-compass exercises, lifesaving techniques, and first aid. We took tests, too. Our intensive field and weapon training required even more study time. I still have two note pads from boot camp, each crammed with notes and information that made good resources for writing this book.

My first Marine haircut was an event to remember. A brief event. Our platoon lined up about 0900 in front of the barber shop. The four barbers had our platoon—all 60 of us—done by 0915. That distinctive Marine haircut took less than a minute per head.

"Those weren't barbers," one of the ranchers from South Dakota observed. "They were sheepshearers." Bernie Watson knew what he was talking about because his family raised sheep.

SHEEPSHEARERS

Marine barbers are fast. Our first haircut took less than a minute. No time to tell 'em how we wanted our hair styled.

Everyone suddenly looked the same. We were bald. The buzz cut hair is "the great equalizer." They had us. Not much chance of going over the hill. We had to stick it out just to get our respectability back, and that would take most of our time in boot camp. After that scalping, I wore a crew cut for almost ten years.

The pressure of boot camp was taking a toll. Some of the men in my platoon were anxious and rattled by the discipline and the tedious PT. Yet this was all part of the Marine Corps plan. If you could not take it, they wanted to know now. They were shaking a lot of old habits out of us and shaking some men loose from the roster. One man in our company committed suicide. Walter Winchell, the broadcaster, said on the air one time: "If you have a Marine in Korea, write to him. If you have a Marine in boot camp, pray for him." Some critics say that Marine boot camp is too disciplined and tough. Nonsense. It was tough training, to be sure, and the discipline was trying, but tough training and discipline prepares a Marine for war.

For Platoon 391, Korea was just around the corner. There was an urgency in our training. For example, the need for soldiers on the ground in Korea cut our training to 10 weeks rather than the traditional 12 weeks. Boot camp's intense experience creates bonds

Recruits were keep busy assembling M1 rifles and with weapons training. Every Marine is a rifleman.

of comradeship so strong that Marines will let nothing stand in their way. In comparing the U.S. Army's basic training to the Marine Corps' boot camp, a good friend, also from Minneapolis, admitted his basic training was more like a "country club." Jack Brask, who served in the Army in the 1950s, admitted he went often to the Post Exchange with buddies for a beer and a hamburger….er, I mean ice cream and candy. No such "boogie bait" for the Marines. We were quarantined, so to speak.

Both Marine officers and NCOs (Noncommissioned Officers) have leadership qualities. This is evident on the battlefield and in boot camp. During boot camp, a few of the recruits in Platoon 391 resisted discipline and took personal offense at some orders. The drill instructor, understanding human nature and psychology, quickly squared away the misguided. The DI was not punishing. He was leading. If leadership is helping others perform at a higher level, then the Marine Corps is pretty good at fostering leadership.

One of the threads that connects all Marines is weapons training. Every Marine is a rifleman. This meant becoming well-acquainted with pistols, M1 rifles, carbines, Browning Automatic Rifles (BARs), machine guns and hand grenades. We spent countless hours on the rifle range. Each Marine must qualify with the M1 semi-automatic Garand Rifle, the weapon General George Patton called the greatest battle implement ever devised. The three qualifying levels are like rankings of good, better, or best: Marksman, Sharp Shooter, and Expert. Despite my weak right eye, I made the Marksman category. This shared expertise or unity assures the Marine Corps of capable fill-ins on the battle front when needed. It happened often in Korea. Combat Correspondents to cooks had to serve up on the front lines as riflemen, BAR men, and machine gunners. One of my fellow Combat Correspondents, Sgt. Frank Kerr, was more rifleman than photographer

Muddy but happy Marines after completing their infiltration course training at Camp Mathews Rifle Range, California, 1952. Author is standing, right. (Author's Collection)

Some of the Texans couldn't get the hang of swimming. But the Marines had a good teacher — a 20-foot diving tower.

during the early battles in 1950. When he shot photos, he was terrific at that, too. Many of the pictures that he took at Inchon and the Chosin Reservoir can be found in the National Archives.

Because of the Marine Corps' amphibious capabilities and assignments all over the world, recruits had to learn how to swim. Marines were first known as "soldiers of the sea," after all. About two weeks into our training, Sgt. Fuller announced that we would take our first of five swimming lessons. Even those who could already swim had to participate in the weekly swimming practice at a gigantic outdoor pool with a tall diving tower on one end. Several Texans could not learn how to swim. God knows they tried. During the last lesson, we had to climb the 20-foot tower and jump into the water. Pvt. Andy Rogers, a Texan, would not jump. He had to be pushed. As he hit the water, my buddy, Dave Maupin, from Springfield, Missouri, commented: "What if he doesn't come up?"

Sgt. Fuller heard him and replied: "Keep watching. He'll come up. They always do. We haven't lost one yet." He was right. When Rogers surfaced he started dog-paddling for his life. Then he settled down and moved his arms more slowly, and, thankfully, stayed above the water. He qualified and was considered a swimmer. Weeks later, Rogers showed some of us up at Camp Henderson's rifle range, where he won an expert badge. To keep him humble, we reminded him of his swimming experience.

The pressure of boot camp got to Billy Daniels, who was in my squad and sleeping quarters. After the third day he said he was going to "get out of this chicken outfit." He went to Sgt. Fuller's Quonset hut and pounded on the door. "Permission to see the Drill Instructor, sir," he shouted.

TOO YOUNG

One of the recruits was only 16 and too young to serve. He wished he hadn't fessed up to the DI, who really fixed him good.

"Permission granted," the sergeant replied. "Now, whatyawant?" he asked the young recruit. The good-looking rookie, tall, blond, and Scandinavian, entered the tiny, neat-as-a-pin office. Intimidated by the DI's cold greeting, he was shaking, but determined.

"Sir! I lied about my age. I'm only 16," Daniels blurted out.

Unfazed, Sgt. Fuller replied, "Well, private, we'd better do something about this. Shouldn't we?" Everyone knew you had to be 17 and have your parents' permission to enlist.

"Yes sir! We need to get me out of the Marines. I'm too young to serve."

"Okay, private. We'll start the paper work. Meanwhile, go back to your barracks. And, oh, be sure to take part in all our activities—until we clear up this little mess. Understood?"

"Yes sir!" Daniels gave a snappy salute and did a perfect about-face and returned to his sleeping quarters. I was there when he got back. He looked relieved, like he had just given a confession of murder to his priest. What a load off his mind. He thought he was going home real soon. "No more of this bull crap for me," he touted to the guys in Platoon 391.

Then the days passed. Everyday he asked Sgt. Fuller if the papers came through. The sergeant, just as po-

The author, left, and Les Johnson, with fixed bayonets at Camp Mathews Rifle Range, California, March 1952. (Author's Collection)

lite as he could be, and with a straight face, informed the reluctant recruit that the papers had not yet come down from the Colonel's office.

Poor Billy Daniels. Day after day, week after week, he endured training with us. Every day he inquired about his discharge papers. They finally "came in" on the day before Platoon 391 graduated from boot camp. For 10 weeks—minus one day—he was a full-time recruit. We later learned that the Colonel had signed the papers the day after the incident was reported, but they sat in the DI's desk drawer to teach the 16-year-old kid a lesson. Had he said nothing, he would have graduated with us and made Pfc. Good Lord! He would have to take boot camp all over again, or some other kind of basic training, when he was of legal age to be in the service.

Years later I learned from a seasoned gunny sergeant that many Marines "snuck in" during World War II when they were 16, or in some cases, even younger. I know one who celebrated his 17th birthday on Iwo Jima. Some of these "Marine babies" were the most gung ho Marines of all.

I was drafted into the Marines. To help fill the ranks, the Marines in the 1950s received a quota of men from selective service. I was among the very few diverted from the Army to the Marines. I was drafted in November 1951 and was in the Minneapolis Federal Building ready to be processed with 40 other selective-service inductees when a John Wayne-looking Marine in a dress blue uniform entered the room. He shouted to the Army Master Sgt. in charge of the inductees, "You don't get 'em all. The Marines get their quota—seven of them."

"Okay," replied the Army sergeant. "But you don't get to hand pick 'em. It has to be random. Here. Pick from their draft notices."

He pulled out my notice. That meant San Diego boot camp for me. Instead of a four-year hitch, as for the regular Marines, I was in for only two years with a six-year reserve obligation. Looking back, it was a lucky day when I was picked out for the Marines. I always admired them. During our fourth week of training, Sgt. Fuller compared regular enlistees to the selective-service guys. As good as the enlistees were, we draftees won. We were older—22 vs. 17 or 18 years old—and more experienced than the younger enlistees. Most of us had been to college. We were better at map problems, better able to reassemble an M1 rifle, better skilled in combat principles, better able to recite our general orders, more knowledgeable about Marine history and traditions, and pretty snappy at close order drills. More importantly, however, we were all Marines.

Sometimes the Marines are dealt some duds. The three recruits from Puerto Rico did not last long in the Marines. After a week of boot camp they claimed they were ill. So, off they went to the sick bay. Navy doctors found the three recruits fit for duty. They reported back to Platoon 391, but refused to drill and would not take orders of any kind. It was obvious that they had planned their ruse from the first day they were drafted and sent to the Marines instead of the Army.

WHERE'S YOUR MUSTACHE?

Boot camp gives you a tremendous appetite. That's where I developed my healthy milk habit. It was cold and refreshing. And you could have as much as you wanted.

Tent buddies at Camp Pendleton, California, 1952. Author in top row, center. (Author's Collection)

They were court-martialed, ruled incorrigible, and received undesirable discharges. Unbothered, they were sent back home.

For me, the Marine experience was invaluable. It was not easy, but training to be the best never is. In boot camp we learned to push ourselves until we thought we were drained, then we found and tapped a reserve we did not know existed. Exceeding limits is part of what being a Marine is all about. We also learned how to function as a member of a very elite team, a team that relies on an individual's instincts and on his ability to make the members of that team perform as one. We developed self-confidence and team-confidence.

Our DIs taught us discipline. A disciplined man is tough-minded, not tough-mannered. True discipline starts with self-control, with the head, not the hands. Discipline is orderly thinking. Concentration. Character. Determination and dedication. Corporal Richard Bolstad, a neighbor of mine from Minneapolis, said, "The discipline I learned from the Marine Corps was exactly what I needed." Bolstad landed at Inchon, earned a Purple Heart, came home, then volunteered for another tour of duty in Korea. He went on to become one of the best vice-squad cops Minneapolis ever had. We are all better off for the discipline the Marine Corps instilled in Bolstad.

We all need discipline, or we become like a rudderless ship. Discipline is exactly what every good author, playwright or composer has realized and lived by. It is the core of a Winston Churchill, and our own Korean War hero, Lt. General Lewis B. "Chesty" Puller. Plus, discipline is part of every man and woman wearing a Marine Corps uniform.

At boot camp we got pushed. And we pushed. We learned how to deal with extraordinary situations that required us to use all our resources and skills. We grew as individuals. Each day we began to understand what an honor it was to participate in a tradition that has endured more than 200 years, a tradition reflected in the memorable motto of the Marine Corps—*Semper Fidelis*, "Always Faithful."

My drill instructors—sergeants N.H. Clyde, H.J. Fuller and P.B. Peters—probably do not remember me or my Platoon 391 partners. We sure remember them. They trained us and thousands like us. They drilled and challenged us. They even set us back on our heels a few times, but all in the name of getting us ready for what lay ahead in Korea. They trained us right. They forged and steeled us as Marines in the boot factory.

AULD LANG SYNE

"So long, drill instructors. It's been good to know you."

A Navy corpsman (no weapon), and Marines carry a wounded lineman to a forward aid station, August 4, 1950. South Korean Service Corps helper follows. (Marine Corps Photo/ Sgt. Frank Kerr)

3

THE UN'S WORST NIGHTMARE

"You are about to take over the most impossible job on earth!"

I was in Korea when those words were spoken by Norway's Trigve Lie to his Swedish successor, Dag Hammarskjold, the new United Nations Secretary-General. It was April 9, 1953. The UN was only eight years old and ill-equipped to run a war the magnitude of the Korean War. Trigve Lie, the first UN Secretary-General, had had enough. He decided to step down. From my vantage point as a Marine Radio Correspondent, it was clear that the United Nations was in the midst of a serious crisis. Korea was the UN's worst nightmare.

True to his Truman Doctrine, in which the U.S. would check the spread of communism in the post-war era, President Harry Truman called for a "police action." The incident brought a new "player" to the table. Enter the United Nations. The Korean War was the first war in which a world organization played a major role. It was the most severe test the United Nations had to face since its inception in 1945. As part of the Cold War scenario, the Korean War was a complicated issue. The UN had to successfully deal with it or lose credibility just five years after it had come into being. In June 1950, North Korean troops unexpectedly attacked South Korea. America wanted the invasion immediately brought before the UN's Security Council.

At the end of World War II, Korea was effectively split in two. The south was in the hands of the United States while Russia dominated the north. The UN had already involved itself in the affairs of Korea when in 1947, before partition, it had declared its intentions that elections should be held for a government for the whole country. The UN wanted to oversee the elections to ensure that they were

That date changed the lives of thousands of young men and women. Me included. It marked the invasion of South Korea and triggered the Korean War.

fair. Not surprisingly, the Russians would not allow United Nations observers in North Korea to observe the elections. (I remember studying some of this at Central High School, in Minneapolis.) By the end of 1948 both North and South Korea had formed separate states. The North was supported by communist Russia. China became a partner when it became communist in 1949 under Mao. South Korea was supported by America and was considered by the west to be the only democratic nation out of the two. Both governments claimed the right to govern the other.

The actual invasion of South Korea took place on June 25, 1950. The UP (United Press) wire service machine was really working overtime. It had reported that the UN's Security Council met the same day. The Russian delegation to the Security Council did not attend the meeting since it was boycotting the UN for recognizing Chiang Kai-shek's government in Taiwan as the official voice for China and ignoring Mao's communist regime in Beijing. Therefore, the obvious use of the veto—which it is assumed the USSR would have used in this case—did not occur. (We had many calls to the station from worried listeners inquiring if the reports meant war for the United States. It did.)

At the UN meeting, America claimed that North Korea had broken world peace by attacking South Korea. We called on North Korea to withdraw to the 38th parallel. Nine out of the eleven countries in the Security Council supported this view. Russia was absent and one abstained. On June 27, two days after the invasion, America called on the United Nations to use force to get the North Koreans out of South Korea, as they had ignored the Security Council's resolution of June 25. This was also voted for. Still boycotting, Russian again could not use its veto. (What a mistake for Russia to miss the meetings.)

United Nations flag. The Korean War was the first war in which a world organization played a major role. (Author's Collection)

The United Nations, led by the Secretary-General, Norway's Trigve Lie, now had to formulate its plans. By now, North Korean troops reached the outskirts of Seoul. President Harry Truman ordered U.S. Air and Naval forces to South Korea. The UN asked its other members to unify with the U.S. and aid South Korea. Sixteen member countries would provide troops under a United Nations Joint Command. The UN Force was primarily dominated by the United States, even being commanded by an American general, Douglas MacArthur. His official title: Commander-in-Chief, United Nations Command.

At first glance it would almost appear the United Nations forces held an unfair advantage in disciplining North Korea for its violation at the 38th parallel. It is obvious now that the North Koreans knew they had some reserve power up their sleeves: that of their next-door neighbors, the Communist Chinese, with additional support from the Russians. Besides the United States and the United Kingdom (Great Britain), there were 16 other countries offering assistance against the communist aggression. They were Australia, Belgium, Canada, Columbia, Denmark, Ethiopia, France, and Greece. Others were Italy, Luxembourg, the Netherlands, Norway, the Philippines, Sweden, Thailand, and Turkey.

LIFESAVERS

Without concern for their own safety, Navy Corpsmen treated wounded Marines on the battlefield and in aid stations. Medics are high on the chain of Marines' favorite people.

Not all countries volunteered ground troops or weapons. Some sent medical aid only. But the UN welcomed this gesture as it needed all the help it could muster. Those sending the medical assistance were the Scandinavians: Denmark (hospital ship), Norway (Mobile Army Surgical Hospital), and Sweden (general hospital.)

The enemy was well aware who was carrying the lion's share of the load for the UN forces. It was the United States, hands down. We supplied 90 percent of the ground troops, 93 percent of all air power and 86 percent of all naval power. The U.S. units participating were as follows:

- U.S. Eighth Army and major units
- U.S. Navy
- U.S. Air Force
- U.S. Marine Corps (First Marine Division and First Marine Air Wing)
- U.S. Coast Guard
- CIA (Central Intelligence Agency)

I was not aware that the U.S. Marine Corps was nearly wasted—not by any enemy—but by the politics in Washington. Some of our regulars, during late-night discussions in our PIO Radio tent, remembered the earlier cutbacks faced by President Truman's cabinet and the Joint Chiefs of Staff. It was no secret that some of the military decision makers had strongly disliked the USMC.

Our older Marines—the historians, if you will—even had the numbers. They said Truman's people had cut the Fleet Marine Force to 34,000 officers and men. It left a ground-fighting strength of only six infantry battalions and a total Corps strength of less than 75,000 officers and men. Eliminated were the two Marine divisions which would have surely helped the United Nations forces in the early days of the war.

During those early weeks in Korea, the first allied offensive of the Korean War, the thin ranks of Marines soon proved that the war was far from over. According to fellow Combat Correspondent Frank Kerr, who was there, the Marines' dash and daring raised morale throughout the country. Kerr, a photojournalist, went on to say that the North Koreans were terrified of the "yellow legs," referring to the Marines' canvas leggings.

The Marine Brigade was pulled out of combat and ordered back to Pusan to board ships. They would join the First Marine Division for the Inchon landing, General Douglas MacArthur's masterful surprise attack far behind enemy lines. Maybe to the distaste of President Truman, MacArthur insisted on using the Marines for what they do best—lead an amphibious assault.

President Truman, realizing the scope of the war, eventually permitted calling up our reserves. The Marines were once again ready for decisive counter-attack behind enemy lines. The total number of Marines in the Korean conflict rose to 130,000.

After the successful Inchon landing on September 15, 1950, the UN forces advanced across the 38th parallel into North Korea, despite the warnings from Communist China. Many historians have written that

RESERVES CALLED

U.S. reservists were activated after North Korea's siege in Seoul. It brought the USMC back to military strength.

Scuttlebutt said the military was going home for Christmas 1950. But the Red Chinese spoiled the idea. Sadly, many men never made it home for any holiday.

if we had stayed in South Korea—that is, stayed south of the 38th parallel—then North Korea, the enemy, may have conceded. It was at this point that things were rolling well for the United Nations. General MacArthur even predicted that the UN forces would be home by Christmas. I remember reading the "Home by Christmas" announcement at my radio station in Eau Claire, Wisconsin. "My, what a short war," I thought to myself. Many of our Marines sent this message home to their loved ones, including my neighbor, Cpl. Richard Bolstad, during his first tour of duty in Korea. (He went back in 1952.)

During the latter part of September, the U.S. Eighth Army was reinforced by a battalion each of Philippine and Australian troops. Early in October, the U.S. Third Division arrived in the Far East. The UN's objective was to keep pushing the North Korean soldiers farther north and at the same time capture industrial and communications areas, port installations, and power and irrigation plants of northeastern Korea. The First Marine Division moved 50 miles north of Hamhung and its port of Hungnam, then turned inland toward the Changin (Chosin) Reservoir, 45 miles to the northwest. Elements of the U.S. Army's Seventh Division attacked northwestward toward the Pujon Reservoir.

During this UN offensive, some Chinese soldiers were captured among the allied units, including the Marines. All were interrogated. Some captives refused to talk. Others hinted that trouble was ahead for the allies, that there was a huge build-up of their comrades waiting to enter the war. This information was rushed to General MacArthur's headquarters in

Tokyo. Nothing came of it as the G-2 (Intelligence) people discounted the reports. They said there was no Chinese intervention to come; the captured Chinese soldiers were probably deserters. This assessment was simply wrong. Commanders of the Eighth Army and the First Marine Division were essentially told: "Not

Gen. Douglas MacArthur (leather jacket), touring the newly opened Inchon Front on September 19, 1950. With him, left, Maj. Gen. Edward M. Almond, Tenth Corps Commander, Vice Adm. Arthur D. Struble, Fifth Fleet Commander and unidentified Marine driver. The road ahead caused problems and cost MacArthur his job seven months later. (AP Photo/ U.S. Army Signal Corps)

to worry. Just keep attacking north." MacArthur's people may have still been living on the "high" from the pivotal breakthrough at Inchon, but a roller-coaster ride awaited them. The bloody tides of war were to shift. The United Nations' biggest nightmare was just ahead.

One of my fellow combat correspondents witnessed the turning point of the war. He was involved in that downside roller-coaster ride for the UN forces. A Marine Combat Photographer with the First Marine Division, Sgt. Frank Kerr, 20, was at the Chosin Reservoir in November 1950. As those Chinese captives promised, more Chinese were to enter the war. First it was a trickle of men. Neither ground troops nor pilots with the U.S. Air Force or First Marine Air Wing spotted them. Then the trickle of Red Chinese became a "Red Tide," masses of troops that "suddenly" appeared on November 27—Thanksgiving Day. From over the Manchurian border came 120,000 fresh Chinese soldiers in 10 divisions. They swept toward 15,000 bone-

Cpl. Charles Price sounds "Taps" over the graves of fallen Leathernecks during memorial services at the 1st Marine Division cemetery at Hungnam, Korea, December 13, 1950. (Marine Corps Photo/Cpl. W.T. Wolfe)

tired Marines and a regimental combat team from the Army's Seventh Infantry Division.

This was more than the UN's Secretary-General could stomach. It was the beginning of the end for Norway's Trigve Lie. A little Monday morning quarterbacking: If the Chinese had not entered the war, then the UN Forces would have needed to only control North Korea, and both General Douglas MacArthur and the United Nations Secretary-General Trigve Lie may have become world class heroes. As it turned out, one got fired and the other retired before the war ended. On April 11, 1951, President Truman relieved General MacArthur of all his commands because of differences over national policy and military strategy. (Dismissed for irreverence to the President and missing the call on the Chinese Communists' intervention.) General Matthew Ridgeway became the Supreme Commander of Allied Powers and James A. Van Fleet assumed command of the Eighth Army on April 14, replacing Ridgeway. Trigve Lie held on a little longer. He remained the United Nations' Secretary-General until April 9, 1953 when Dag Hammarskjold replaced him.

Years later when I was back in Minnesota, some Swedes chided their Norwegian neighbors about the UN's Trigve Lie, who was from Norway. "See! It took a Swede to end the war." Yes, Dag Hammarskjold was from Sweden. And yes, there's still a friendly, but ongoing rivalry among the Scandinavians in Minnesota.

Many historians suggest that had we stayed south of the 38th parallel, many lives may have been saved.

THE GENERAL'S FOLLY

The public turned against President Harry Truman for firing General Douglas MacArthur. As brilliant a strategist as he was, the general was dead-wrong about the Red Chinese Army's role in the war. History shows that Truman made the right call.

The Chinese warned us about going past the line separating the two Koreas.

Korea has been called one of the bloodiest and costliest wars in modern history. Here is the price of the UN's worst nightmare:

Korean War Casualties (rounded out)

- United Nations Command—500,000 casualties (94,000 killed)
- United States Units (Combined)—99,000 casualties (54,000 deaths)
- U.S. Marines—30,000 casualties (5,500 deaths)
- South Korea—ROK Army and civilians—Over one million killed
- The Enemy (North Korea and China)—Between 1.25 and 1.5 million killed, wounded, captured prisoners or missing

I was in Korea during President-elect Dwight D. Eisenhower's "secret" visit to Korea. He flew there on November 29, 1952. He was slated to stop at the First Marine Division headquarters, where I was at the PIO Radio Section. He did not make it since his trip was cut short due to security reasons. He spent some time close by at Panmunjom with the United Nations negotiators. While there he also conferred with the top Marines, knowing their key involvement in the war. As a result of his peace-seeking mission, an armistice was signed in July 1953, eight months after his trip.

To this day, I feel that former president Eisenhower had much to do with the closure of the war. Under the terms of the Armistice signed in Panmunjom, the two Koreas were separated by a demilitarized zone (DMZ)

WE LIKE IKE

President-elect Dwight D. Eisenhower visited Korea in 1952. His presence at the truce table helped end the war.

at the 38th parallel, roughly the same border that existed prior to the war.

The war was seen as proof that the United Nations could be counted on to resist aggression, and that modern warfare could be conducted without resorting to nuclear weapons. In retrospect, maybe we should have. Many a Miller, Budweiser, and Coors have been shared by Marines while discussing the Korean War. What used to bug Bob Fugate, former MSgt. combat writer in my PIO section, was the outcome.

"What a lousy ending," Fugate used to start with. "No one won. No wonder they call it The Forgotten War."

He was right. The Marines were not used to that kind of warfare. Duane Knops, a colleague of mine and a veteran of Iwo Jima, probably said it best. "There was no winner in Korea. At least on Iwo Jima, the Marines got to raise a flag."

NO WINNER

No one won the Korean War. It became the "forgotten war." As an Iwo Jima veteran said: "At least we got to raise a flag on Iwo Jima in WWII."

Sgt. Angelo R. Caramico, combat photographer, found himself a target for a sniper, January 9, 1952. He attempted to get photos of an "empty" enemy bunker, still occupied by the Communists. During the scramble, the New York City Marine got to safer ground. But sniper fire hit the bed of his camera, as the bullet hole shows. (Marine Corps Photo/MSgt. W.A. Rull)

4

COMBAT
CORRESPONDENTS

Combat Correspondents (CCs) are part of Public Affairs, the most powerful public relations team in the military. During my stint in Korea, 1952–1953, the designation was Public Information Office (PIO). Combat Correspondents are skilled in mass communications. The CC team includes journalists, photographers, motion picture, radio-television broadcasters, artists, illustrators and related professionals. They are bold and talented military adventurers who risk their lives to get their story. More than forty CCs died in combat in WWII and subsequent actions. There is no other organization in the military that stacks up to Marine Combat Correspondents. Their history and accomplishments are legendary.

Our CC mission during the Korean War was simple: Tell the Marine Corps story for the folks back home.

Garry M. Cameron wrote the granddaddy of all Combat Correspondent books, *Last to Know, First to Go* (published by the United States Marine Corps Combat Correspondents Association in 1988). Below is an excerpt about how the Combat Correspondents came to be.

In the Beginning

Early in 1941, many career Marines were shocked when they heard the rumor that the Corps was going to activate a Public Relations Division.

"Public relations? What the hell is that?" was the question posed by those who would soon be training thousands of young men to serve in their beloved Corps.

Brig. Gen. Robert Denig led the charge before WWII to organize a public relations unit. It was a new venture for the Marines.

"Means something to do with the telling the civilians about us. Crap! Give us a mission and the public will know about it soon enough!"

It was not a rumor and on June 30, 1941, the framed statement, IF THE PUBLIC BECOMES APATHETIC ABOUT THE MARINE CORPS, THE MARINE CORPS WILL CEASE TO EXIST, was placed on the wall above the desk of the first director of a Marine Corps Public Relations Division. Colonel Robert L. Denig, USMC, retired after 36 years service, was given a so-called tombstone promotion to brigadier general, then recalled to active duty and ordered to take charge of this new staff agency.

Like most Marines at that time, Denig knew nothing about public relations and freely admitted it to the Commandant, Major General Thomas Holcomb, with whom he had served in France during World War I.

"You had better learn about it," warned the Commandant, "because that is what you are going to be." Admittedly puzzled about his assignment, Gen. Denig walked into his office, an inside storage room lit only by a dirty light bulb. His staff was waiting for him and First Sergeant Walter J. Shipman introduced the general to his two civilian clerks, Lorene Lomax and Helen Draper. Little did this small group of novices realize then that, in less than four years, the Division at Headquarters, Marine Corps and overseas would grow to 268 officers and enlisted Marines.

When Pearl Harbor exploded into World War II, Gen. Denig saw the need for combat reporters. He and his First Sergeant, Walter J. Shipman, agreed that newspaper publishers would be the best place to look for experienced reporters and photographers. The goal was ten experienced newsmen. Then another ten would be added. Gen. Denig left the details up to Shipman. (First sergeants have a way of meeting goals and challenges.) Shipman prepared for the mission by putting on his dress blue uniform and decorations. Next, he went to the city editors for permission to talk to their personnel. Then, in recruiting the people, Shipman's biggest selling point was *combat duty*. The prospects liked what they heard and saw. They could not keep their eyes off Shipman's dress blues and medals. The Marine recruiter realized that he was hitting their hot button when he described the job as "reporters for combat duty." Eventually the name combat reporter graduated to "combat correspondent," as it is known today.

COMBAT DUTY

A chance to be an eyewitness and report WWII was the big selling point for the first combat correspondents. Press people are adventurers and like to cover the big stories.

Shipman did a whale of a selling job. The former assistant editor of the *Washington Post*, Sam Stavisky, agrees. He recalled the incident in *Last to Know, First to Go:*

"By word of mouth, it went around town that a Marine by the name of Shipman was trying to recruit newspapermen as CCs in the Marine Corps and the idea sounded good." In March 1942, Stavisky told a friend he was interested in the program. The next thing he knew, Shipman was in his office, literally wooing him for the Corps.

When the Marine Commandant, Gen. Holcomb, asked Denig where he got the ten combat reporters, the written answer replied: "Oh, I just sent Sgt. Shipman over to town." Shipman went to town in more ways than one. He virtually stripped every news room in Washington, D.C.

The first correspondents came from major dailies, small-town weeklies, Hollywood studios and small-town radio stations.

Cissie Patterson, owner of the *Times-Herald*, complained to President Roosevelt about the loss of her reporters. FDR passed the matter on to Gen. Holcomb, who called in Denig. Shipman recalls, "Damned if I didn't have to see the Commandant," and Gen. Denig was ordered to canvas for CC's elsewhere than the District of Columbia's newspapers.

Shipman signed up twenty experienced news people to kick off the Marines' newest unit, the Combat Correspondents. This first group became known as Denig's Demons. They came from major dailies and small-town weeklies, from Hollywood studios and small-town radio stations in the Midwest. After boot camp and combat training, they began to appear in the field. Their mission was to tell the Marine Corps' story for the folks back home. Gen. Denig believed the best way to tell the story was through the eyes of a Marine. The CCs emphasized the individual deeds and accomplishments of Marines. The so-called big picture was left to other media.

In May of 1952 I arrived in Korea and joined the Combat Correspondent team at PIO Headquarters, First Marine Division. My Military Occupational Specialty (MOS) read: *"4313/Broadcast Journalist—Radio Announcer."* I was 21, a corporal, ready, able and eager to record the Korean War. I was the rookie joining the experienced pros, including a mix of regulars, reservists, and career Marines. Many had served in World War II.

First to greet me was MSgt. Joseph Hensley, a noncommissioned officer (NCO) in charge of Radio Correspondents. A career Marine, he was my supervisor. Another radio CC was Jack Latham, from my hometown of Minneapolis. Others included MSgt. Robert E. Johnson, PIO Section Chief. Johnson was a career Marine from Kohler, Wisconsin. Others on deck were MSgt. Robert Fugate and SSgt. D. Martin, writers, and MSgt. H.B. Wells and TSgt. R. Kiser, photographers. We also had two artists from *Leatherneck* magazine, SSgt. Stan Dunlap and Sgt. John Chalk. In the fall of 1952, Capt. Bem Price joined us as the Division PIO commanding officer. He was a reservist and had been covering the Korean War as a journalist for the Associated Press (AP). Now he was wearing a Marine Corps uniform and heading up PIO Headquarters. What a team! I was impressed.

Radio, my bag, was a media workhorse during the Korean War. Television had not earned its stripes yet. Vietnam was the first "TV War," and was more than ten years away. Unlike the printed words of newspapers, radio was more personal, featuring the human voice. Radio could get to the minds of people. For stories, I traveled by jeep, truck, and helicopter all over the division. Often recording in the war zone, I huddled in trenches with real heroes on the firing line. Once I took a dinghy out to a hospital ship—the USS *Haven*—to interview Capt. Ted Williams, the baseball Hall of Famer. The story was broadcast nationally and caused quite a stir. (See the chapter entitled *Ted Williams' Close Call.*)

What were the tools and equipment of a radio correspondent in Korea? Our recording equipment was cumbersome, old technology, but the broadcast qual-

"HONEY, I REENLISTED!"

To pay for his honeymoon, Stan Dunlap signed up for another four-year hitch. But he didn't tell his bride until after the wedding. Like the rest of us, he was soon headed for Korea— without his bride.

ity was excellent. We used the Webcor Brand Recorder that was made in Chicago. Unlike today's ultra-slim recorders, mine weighed close to 50 pounds. For power, when recording in the field, it required an equally heavy Briggs and Stratton portable generator.

Combat Correspondents at PIO Division Headquarters, March 1953. The author, lower left, SSgt. Stan Dunlap, right. Top row, left to right: SSgt. D. Martin, TSgt. Robert Kiser (in T-shirt) and with mustache, MSgt. Harold B. Wells. (Author's Collection)

The manufacturer's description of "portable" was a misnomer. That baby was heavy. For fuel we lugged a five-gallon gas can. Equally heavy was the 100-foot heavy-duty extension cord, used to separate the noisy generator from the microphone.

We always packed extra rolls of 3M Scotch Brand reel-to-reel audio tape. The tape, by the way, held up for over 50 years. Audio tape is expected to "fall apart" after being stored for a long time, but the sound remained amazingly clear. This is not a paid endorsement, but 3M is professional grade. Their audio tape performed, despite the rough field conditions. (Greatapes Recording Studio in Minneapolis could not believe how good the quality was. For transcript purposes, they dubbed the Ted Williams interview—and others—onto a CD in preparation for this book.) For maintenance, ourtool box held pliers, screwdrivers, and plenty of electrician's tape for the many times our extension cord would get shot up. For personal protection I wore my helmet and flak jacket (an armored vest), and wherever I went, I carried my M1 rifle.

Radio Correspondents perform diverse tasks. My responsibilities included:

PIO Radio Projects

- Conduct "Joe Blow" interviews for hometown radio stations
- Provide monthly feature stories to *Marine Corps Radio Show*
- Supply spot-news stories to news services for distribution to newspapers and stations

HOOKED ON MAIL

Once you get used to receiving letters from home, you expect them. When they don't come, well, OUCH! Keep that mail flowing to loved ones and friends in the military. And put in a picture or two. And maybe some cookies.

MSgt. Joe Hensley after a front-line recording session, 1953. (Photo Courtesy Joe Hensley)

- Fulfill special media requests for radio networks and major stations

Secondary Duties

- Media Escort
- Reporter for *The First Word*, First Division's daily newspaper
- Special Assignments

Working with a supervisor you respect is a pleasure. It becomes a double pleasure when you like the supervisor, too. A career Marine, MSgt. Joe Hensley, my boss, racked up 28 years of service. He was in uniform during World War II, Korea, and Viet Nam. Well-skilled in broadcast journalism, Joe made sure that our radio stories had listener appeal. He would not accept mediocre performance. As a teacher, he raised the bar higher and higher. Joe's secret was constructive criticism. He helped me grow in radio.

With nearly three decades in PIO and Public Affairs, Joe pulled some dream assignments. Joe was involved with the blockbuster movie *South Pacific*, starring Mitzi Gaynor, Rossano Brazzi, and John Kerr. In Hollywood, he was technical advisor to the movie studios and advised anyone working on a script or planning to do a movie involving the Marines. Years earlier, he played himself as a Marine in Jack Webb's *The DI*, one of the first and best films about Marines in boot camp.

Our top gun at PIO Headquarters in Korea was Capt. Bem Price. A reservist and a top-notch journalist with the Associated Press, the Corps called him back to active service. As a journalist with AP, he was already reporting on the Korean War. After intensive training stateside, the Corps named him commanding officer of PIO in Korea in October 1952. Price was detailed, disciplined, organized, and smart. He was knowledgeable in all facets of communications. He helped build a special relationship between the media and Marines. Like an experienced ringmaster, he was able to manage the media circus that the Korean War became. The PIO staff and Combat Correspondents bought into his winning program. He often said, "The fun in life is winning."

BEM'S GEMS

Capt. Bem Price had some of the best writers, photographers, radio and press staff in the Corps. I learned a lot from them as they were willing to share their expertise.

During World War II, when the Marine Public Relations and its Combat Correspondents program was getting started, Colonel Robert L. Denig, founder, called his team, "Denig's Demons." Ten years later in Korea, not to be outdone, or go without a nickname, our PIO section was known as "Bem's Gems." But we never wanted Bem Price to hear that. The CCs in Price's command were skilled specialists, real movers and shakers in their jobs. Price had some of the best writers, photographers, radio staff, and press staff in the Corps, including Dick Arnold, Bill Coleman, J.E. Cox, Bill Daum, Bob Fugate, Bob Johnson, R. Kiser, D. Martin, Greg Pearson, Walt Swindells, and H.B. Wells. On the radio side there was Joe Hensley, Jack Latham and me.

Since Price and his key people were busy administering, problem-solving, and playing host to the news media and visiting VIPs, some escort assignments fell to the CCs. This was a nice change of pace for us, and a chance to learn how the big-time reporters did it. Some of the famous reporters that came to Korea were Walter Cronkite, Marguerite Higgins, James A. Michener, Edward R. Murrow, and others.

A GOOD READ

Last to Know, First to Go
 - *Garry M. Cameron*

One Bugle No Drums
 - *William B. Hopkins*

The Outpost War
 - *Lee Ballenger*

SOS Korea 1950
 - *Raymond Maurstad*

The Coldest War and The Scariest Place in the World
 - *James Brady*

One project that kept our radio section humping was the Hometown Radio Tapes series. These "Joe Blow" interviews were the backbone of the Combat Correspondents' system. The format was simple. A Marine identified himself, gave his rank and hometown, then delivered a short message to family members or friends. Joe Hensley, who spearheaded and coordinated the program, said it was one of the most gratifying projects during his 28 years in the Marines. Over 1,000 interviews were recorded during his tour of duty in Korea. Can you imagine a mother's surprise when she heard her boy's voice speaking from Korea? Or a young lady's excitement when her fiancé or boyfriend was featured on the radio? The talking letters ran only about a minute, but they provided lasting memories for the listener. Most were recorded in the battalion reserve areas; some from medical aid tents. Here is one that I remember recording with a Pfc. rifleman from Fargo, North Dakota. His message to his girlfriend, Bonnie, was a love letter, of sorts. No stage fright, he grabbed the microphone and identified himself. Then said:

———————————

Hi, Bonnie. I hope you didn't forget about me, because I sure haven't forgotten about you. Even the guys in my squad know a lot about you. They saw your pictures and think you're swell. That offer to work on your Dad's farm, when I get back, sounds liked a good idea to me. That way, I get to see a whole lot more of you. I can hardly wait to get home and pick up where we left off. Hope you feel the same way. Keep sending those good pictures of yourself. I've got them hanging in my bunker. They sure add a lot to it. When I see them, I want to come home. I'd like to say a whole lot more, but they'd probably censor it. See you soon. Say hello to your folks. Keep writing. My buddies say your letters are the best they've ever read.

MORALE BUILDER

The radio messages from Marines boosted morale for both troops and the public.

Let's hope everything worked out for that North Dakota Marine and his "Bonnie."

The "Joe Blow" tapes were a powerful morale booster for troops and families. They played on hundreds of hometown stations, including WDAY Radio in Fargo, North Dakota, where that young farm girl may have swooned when she heard her Marine hero talk about his future plans with her. After Joe Hensely, Jack Latham and myself recorded the interviews, they were rushed to Marine Corps Headquarters in Quantico, Virginia. An important cog in the wheel at Quantico, was MSgt. William Bierd, from Madison, Wisconsin. Bill Bierd was the best when it came to broadcasting. A career Marine, he had had his own radio program, *Hit the Deck*, that was quite popular when he served in China. Bierd recalled the Hometown Radio project and explained the process:

We received the "Joe Blow" tapes from Korea at our recording studio at Marine Headquarters. Because they were recorded in the field and varied in speed, we first had to correct some to the standard 7 1/2 ips [inches per second] speed. Next, we edited each one to

The author at PIO Radio Section, March 1953. Names on sign: "MSgt. Joe Hensley, SSgt. Jack Latham and Sgt. Dick Hill." (Author's Collection)

make sure it played out well for radio. Now the tape had to be transcribed onto a disc. We logged in the individual's name, hometown and state. Each recording [disc], was forwarded to a Marine Recruiter in the individual's region. In most cases, he hand-delivered it to the radio station [i.e., WDAY Radio, Fargo, N.D.]. Then the station's traffic department would schedule it as a PSA [Public Service Announcement]. Before airing it, the station would contact the Marine's family, to give them the date and time of broadcast. Without exception, stations all over the country cooperated. It was a strong "partnership" the Marines had with the broadcasters and the rest of the media. Looking back, it was a PR coup. A Herculean job, public relations people in the business sector applauded the Marines for pulling it off.

The morale meter jumped substantially when the Hometown Messages were broadcast. The "talking letters," as some called them, made a hit not only with the Marine's family, but the general public as well. Many radio station managers said the messages were the most popular public service series they aired. Today, the military uses the same format for video greetings seen on television, especially around the holiday season.

The demand for radio coverage featuring Marines was non-stop. Besides the traditional "Joe Blow" hometown tapes, we recorded both spot news and feature stories for the media. Plus, the *Marine Corps Show*, on the NBC radio network, required one feature story each month. It aired coast-to-coast on the first Saturday of every month at 8:00 p.m. EST. Broadcast from the beautiful Palladium Ballroom on Sunset Boulevard in Hollywood, California, this prime-time 30-minute program had millions of listeners. A musical-variety show, it spotlighted top musicians and movie stars. Top name bands included Harry James, Les Brown, and Benny Goodman. A few of the film stars on the show were Glenn Ford (a former Marine Combat Correspondent from World War II), Susan Hayward, Judy Garland, Betty Hutton, and the up-and-coming Marilyn Monroe.

Midway through the program was a three-minute tape segment showcasing the Marines in Korea. Unlike a newscast, which features an announcer reading the war news of the day, these tapes for the *Marine Corps Show* "put" the listeners on the front lines of Korea. In many of the recordings you can hear actual rifle and mortar fire in the background. I consider myself fortunate to have provided many of these stories. One of the shows featured the interview with Ted Williams I recorded in April 1953. It caused quite a sensation as Williams was one of the most famous Marines during the Korean War.

These very tapes have since become transcripts and are featured in many chapters in this book. The tapes are an important part of military history. Capt. Daniel Huvan, a Marine Public Affairs officer in New York, calls the recordings that sat in my duffel bag for over 50 years "an historical gold mine." I'm honored to share them with readers.

Our tape recorders had multiple uses in the Korean War. They even became valuable tools for Intelligence

NOW HEAR THIS

I was the activities announcer on the USNS General Walker during the voyage back to the states in 1953. I read the daily announcements from the pilot house on the bridge. About five days into the trip home I found a note on my bunk: "We've had enough of your crappy movie, physical training and duty notices. When do the girls get here?"

SECRET WEAPON

Besides the traditional use for radio broadcasts, our tape recorders were used for diversionary tactics and interviewing the wounded.

officers. Here are two examples. I was on a top secret assignment working with the Division's G-2 (Intelligence) and the First Division tank battalion. It is okay to talk about the assignment now, since many years have passed and the project is declassified. Operation Echo was a diversionary tactic using tanks and my tape recorder. I taped the actual sound of some of the tanks. Then on the following moonless night, the sound from my tape recorder was amplified on huge 20-inch speakers on the front line. As anticipated, the Chinese took the bait, thinking they heard a tank movement. The diversionary tactic kept the Chinese mortar and artillery crews busy while a reconnaissance squad penetrated enemy lines and gathered information from another direction. (See the *Operation Echo* chapter for the full story.)

A second example involved Sgt. Joe Hensley. He was with S-2 Intelligence at the Regiment level. His sleep was interrupted on a cold October night. He left his sleeping bag and dressed quickly as the 7th Regiment wanted Joe and his tape recorder at the battalion aid station. A young corporal had brought wheels for him. During the jeep ride, the driver told Joe that he would interview wounded Marines brought to the aid bunker from the front lines. S-2 officers wanted any intelligence information they could get from the wounded Marines that were attacked on "The Hook," a ridge on the frontlines. "We need more pieces to the puzzle," they told Joe. Days later, Joe heard that much was learned from the wounded riflemen, and more of the puzzle was pieced together.

While Joe was taping interviews, a Corpsman was attending to the wounded and injured while another corpsman was trying to repair a broken Coleman lantern. The electric lines were shot up, so the lights were out and the lantern was a poor substitute. Then a "light" went on in Joe's head. He became a hero that night by supplying electricity from his portable generator that powered our tape recorders. The doctors and corpsmen marveled at Joe's ingenuity. A Navy chaplain, also present in the aid station to comfort the wounded, thanked Joe by asking if he would like his coffee sweetened. He nodded yes. So the chaplain, also ready for emergencies, poured a bit of bourbon from the canteen he was carrying. For medicinal purposes, of course.

We kidded Joe Hensley about the electric light that he rigged up in the aid tent. We told him he was trying to top Rudolph the Red Nosed Reindeer. Rudolph, you may remember, supplied the light that one foggy night, to lead Santa's sleigh. The song, by Gene Autry, was gaining in popularity on our Armed Forces Radio Station. That's what made us think of the tie-in. When we reminded Joe about it, he would merely brush it aside by saying: "Whatever it takes."

The strength of the Combat Correspondents program came from outside and inside the Corps, from schooling and experience from on-the-job training. In our PIO section, for example, Bem Price brought in his experience with the Associated Press, just as I brought in mine from several radio stations. Something else Price had with him, that we all used, was his *Associated Press Style Book*. It is the best in the industry. Many of the career Marines in our section learned their journalism trade from *Leatherneck* magazine. According to MSgt. Bob Fugate, *Leatherneck* was called "the journalism school for writers, photographers and artists." The award-winning magazine had "teachers" who shared their knowledge and helped shape and guide newcomers to journalism success.

I had a chance to see several of *Leatherneck's* disciples in action. Two worked out of our PIO Headquarters in Korea. SSgt. Stan Dunlap and Sgt. John Chalk, combat artists, were on TAD (Temporary Additional Duty) from their home base in Quantico, Virginia. Both were freewheeling and damn-good CCs. They sketched the war as they saw it. Dunlap was also staff artist on the division's newspaper, *The First Word*, while I was a reporter. Starting modestly as a mimeograph publication, the initial circulation was around 900 copies. After the truce was signed in July 1953, the paper ex-

Capt. Bem Price, right, with Col. J.C. Landrum, battalion commander, receives congratulations on his Purple Heart award. Price was wounded on March 28, 1953. He later won the Legion of Merit for "outstanding performance of duties" as divisional Public Information Officer. (Marine Corps Photo)

panded to over 10,000 copies and became a weekly tabloid printed by South Koreans in Seoul. J.E. Cox, editor, was responsible for its expansion.

John Chalk, an illustrator, cartoonist, and sculptor, made quite a name for himself with his art story, "Beyond the Imjin." He sketched the 7th Marines on the frontlines in February of 1953 when the war was still going strong. It was featured in *Leatherneck* later that year and created lots of attention. As a combat artist, Chalk was serving with both the 5th and 7th Regiments. Our paths crossed often as we hitched rides together while on assignments. On one of our get-togethers, Chalk sketched me while I was taping a story on the front lines. A cartoon, it ended up in *Leatherneck* magazine. My grandkids still get a chuckle out of it.

Leatherneck *magazine artist, John Chalk. He and the author crossed paths frequently while performing assignments. (Author's Collection)*

After Chalk's tour in Korea, he considered going for a commission. Don Dickson, publisher and officer in charge of *Leatherneck*, talked him out of it. It would have taken Chalk back to the war zone as a 2nd lieutenant—pure cannon fodder. He took his discharge, but missing the action from Korea, he considered joining the French Foreign Legion. Then his future wife, Mary Diniakos, came along. They have five children and 17 grandchildren and live in Palm Harbor, Florida.

MSgt. Robert Fugate and MSgt. Harold B. (H.B.) Wells made one fantastic news team. Both were career Marines and experienced CCs in our PIO section. H.B. Wells explains their close partnership:

———————————

Bob Fugate and I worked as a journalism team in Korea. He was the writer. I was his photographer.

Combat photographer, MSgt. Harold (H.B.) Wells. He and Bob Fugate, writer, worked as a journalism team. (Author's Collection)

Fugate knew his way around. He had been captured on Bataan in World War II and spent some time in a Japanese prison camp. He was imprisoned long enough so that he picked up the Japanese language. And could speak it as well as I've heard it during my trips to Japan. The war didn't scare him one bit. Even enemy small-arms fire flying all around up on the lines didn't chase him off his assignments as a combat writer. He'd go up and down the MLR (Main Line of Resistance), and ask the riflemen how they were doing. Sometimes the ground pounders didn't want anything to do with Combat Correspondents. But Bob had a way of connecting. They sensed he was OK. He'd have them talking and laughing in no time. He'd get the information he needed and their names. Then had me get the photos of them. "In action," he'd remind me.

It was sure gratifying to see our stories wind up in newspapers and magazines. Including *Leatherneck*. Occasionally we'd split up and go on media escort assignments. We CCs all took the media people around the division for their stories. I spent one year in Korea and I think it's fair to say that Bob Fugate and I earned our combat pay and got our share of war stories for the people back home.

———

Here is one of their stories. It shows the ingenuity of a determined tank crew and the nifty writing style of Fugate. Thanks to Walt Ford, editor, *Leatherneck*, for permission to publish. It ran in March 1953:

Operation Lady – by MSgt. Robert Fugate

WAR IS A SERIES of situations in need of improvement. We had a high hill while the Commies held two neighboring hills. Both of their hills overlooked ours. Our situation was not a happy one—and we wanted to make alterations. We wanted an outpost in front of our position on a little hill called "Lady." The problem of putting a bunker on "Lady" didn't seem to have an easy solution; every time men exposed themselves the Commies cut loose with everything from artillery to small-arms fire.

Captain Leland Graham of the First Battalion, Fifth Marines conceived a direct plan. Simply take a pre-fabricated bunker out to "Lady" and set it up while Marines cover the operation with friendly fire.

Bob Fugate (front) and Joe Hensley served together in Korea and later in Hollywood. Both were master sergeants. (Photo courtesy Joe Hensley)

A tank-dozer—a regular tank fitted with a bull dozer blade—would scoop out a hole for the bunker. Then a tank retriever would take the two-ton, pre-fabricated bunker out and drop it into the hole. Again the tank-dozer would return to the bunker and push the dirt around it. It was a fine plan, but it had to be accomplished while the Commies watched and threw plenty of incoming mail. Aside from the enemy's determination to discourage the operation, the terrain, weather and mechanical difficulties seemed to stack heavy odds against successful completion of the plan.

The Marines tried four times, on four successive days, before they succeeded.

On the first day heavy rains covered the area. The operation was postponed. The second day's attempt proved that the tank-dozer's engine had been fouled by rain water. On the third try, the 'dozer got through to the hill and started to dig. Then the hydraulic system that controlled the 'dozer-blade failed. On the return trip the 'dozer threw one of its treads.

But the fourth try was successful. The 'dozer lumbered out a narrow winding road toward "Lady" and started burrowing into the loose sand on the reverse side. Its calm, deliberate movements seemed incongruous. On the Commie-held hills there were countless artillery pieces that could readily be brought to bear on "Lady." This fact had determined the location of the intended bunker on the reverse slope of the hill. And while the 'dozer worked, enemy mortar fire pounded the forward slope.

When the task of scooping the dirt was completed, everything was in readiness for the second phase of the operation. The 'dozer driver, Corporal Malcolm P. Burns, Jr., lost no time in getting his iron monster back to our lines. He backed down the road, the blade of his machine furnishing additional protection against the artillery and mortar fire being poured in on him by the Chinese.

The retriever came on with its load as soon as the 'dozer had cleared the road. It loomed up on the ridgeline like a pre-historic reptile, the two-ton bunker dangling from its boom.

This part of the operation was precarious. Incoming shells landed closer and closer; there was no time to tarry. Two members of the retriever's crew hung out of their hatches holding heavy guy lines attached to the bunker to keep the bulky object from swaying.

The driver of the retriever, Sergeant William M. Mathieu, drove to the prepared hole and swung the bunker into it as easily as he might have dropped a nickel in a parking meter.

"Operation Lady" was almost completed. The hole had been dug. The bunker had been placed. Now the dirt around the hole had to be pushed back in around the bunker to give it added protection.

Fury seemed to rise in the Commies as they began to realize that the brazen operation promised to be successful. Their artillery, mortar and machine gun fire picked up. Chinese "76s" chased the retriever back to our lines. Friendly fire was passed overhead. Corp. Burns, undismayed by the enemy fire, pulled out again and calmly pushed the needed dirt around the bunker and returned safely to our lines. A bunker had been set up in plain sight of the enemy, and under his fire without losing a man. The only casualty was a portion of the right rear of the tankdozer which had been torn off by a near-miss.

MSgt. Joe Hensley, left, NCO in charge of radio correspondents. (Photo Courtesy Joe Hensley)

The entire operation—from start to finish—took only 90 minutes.

How long would the bunker stay on "Lady?" Certainly the matter would be disputed in days to come, for surely the Commies would try to obliterate our "improvement."

In this chess-game war, we had moved another pawn into the enemy's king-row.

———

Another fellow Combat Correspondent who earned his combat pay was William A. Daum, a writer. He retired as a master sergeant. Here is Bill's accounting of his PIO days in Korea:

———

I joined the First Marine Division PIO in November 1952. Bem Price was officer in charge, Walt Swindells was assistant and Bob Johnson was the non-commissioned officer in charge. My first assignment was up on the lines with photographer Marty Riley. Got some

Bill Daum recalls his days as a combat correspondent, including an episode with an Army captain who tried to sidetrack his mission.

good stuff, but froze our butts off. (Thank God for the hand warmers my wife sent.) Filed copy and photos via the occasional jeep going to Div. Hdq. Covered everything from the Marine hometown stories (Joe Blow interviews), to recon patrols with the ground-pounders and other activities with supporting units. One memory is of the eager S-2 second lieutenant who posted Ed Scullin, photographer, that replaced Riley, on a forward OP (Outpost), in an endeavor to find out where the enemy machine guns were located. The secret: open the lens (this is at night) to detect muzzle flashes.

Joined the 5th Marines after Reno-Vegas-Carson outpost battles in March 1953. Filed the first piece on Francis C. Hammond, a young Medical Corpsman KIA (killed in action) on Vegas while attempting to save Marines. He was awarded the Medal of Honor for his gallantry. Joined Col. Lew Walt for coverage of 105 Purple Heart awards following the operation. Trying to keep tabs (literally) on that many individuals and their pictures for their hometown newspapers was a challenge. (But nothing compared to what they did to win those Purple Hearts.)

In late July, or thereabouts, I was assigned, along with Dick Arnold, to the Munsan-Ni Provisional Command, run by the Army to set up and conduct Operation Big Switch, the POW Exchange. We were the only Marines in the PIO section, which proved rather unnerving to some of our Army compatriots. On one occasion, when told we were to police up the area, Dick and I informed a young Army captain that Marine Staff NCOs do not occupy themselves in such endeavors.

It was a fascinating assignment. We interviewed ex-POWs (Prisoners of War), as they came through processing. Also, assisted the civilian press when need be. (Some of whom I ran into 12 years later in Saigon.) In September 1953 I joined the 7th Marines when we began filing copy on the effects of the truce upon frontline troops. By then, Capt. Verlie Ludwig, headed PIO with 2nd Lt. Bob Morrisey as assistant officer in charge. Some other CCs during my Korean tour included Mel Jones, Greg Pearson, Tim Rattray, Jack Latham, Dick Hill, Bill Coleman, Stan Dunlap and Joe Hensley. Of course we had many photographers, not all named here, before the day of the hi-tech 35mm camera we carried in Vietnam.

BEFORE GPS

How did Marines function without today's Global Positioning System? We did it the hard way with a compass and map. And we were pretty good at it.

Technical Sergeant William Daum received a well-earned combat citation for his service in Korea. Without regard for his personal safety while on patrols far behind the MLR (Main Line of Resistance), Bill did what any good Combat Correspondent would do. He did his job. Further, Bill received a Letter of Commendation from the U.S. Army. He and Dick Arnold were assigned to the Munsan-Ni Provisional command, run by the Army. They were involved in Operation Big Switch, the United Nations POW Exchange.

I think Brigadier General Robert L. Denig, founder of the Marine's Public Affairs operation, would have been proud of Capt. Bem Price's Combat Correspondents in Korea. Our achievements are a matter of record. I was honored to be in his command and to rub elbows with the wonderful mix of CCs—career Marines, regulars and reservists. This was a once-in-a-lifetime experience I will never forget. I will also never forget Bem Price's credo—"The fun in life is winning,"—or Joe Hensley's saying "Whatever it takes."

Marguerite Higgins, New York Herald Tribune, *landing at Suwon, near Seoul, Korea, 1950. After being warned of trouble ahead, she said: "I wouldn't be here if there was no trouble. Trouble is news, and the gathering of it is my job." (Photo Courtesty Doubleday and Company)*

5

THE MEDIA CIRCUS

The Korean War was a "media circus." The term had not been invented yet when I served in Korea. But that is exactly what it was. By all measurements, I know. I was in the middle of it.

Part of my job as a Radio Correspondent was working with the media. And they were coming in by droves to cover America's—and the world's, for that matter—biggest media event in the 1950s. As the Marines held the "hot ticket" in the war, the reporters headed for the First Marine Division Public Information Office Headquarters. During one month alone, nearly 100 reporters logged in.

As part of the PIO section, I was among the many chaperones assigned to the visiting reporters and VIPs. After extending a warm welcome, we would get their housing settled. Sometimes this was nothing more than a sleeping bag in a leaky tent, but they did not mind. Their priority was front-page stories from the Marines' front lines. Before that, they needed to be filled in on the existing situation, attend some briefings, and if necessary, be issued a helmet and flak jacket. Transportation was scarce. When available, we supplied a jeep and the escort service and protection they needed to get around in a war zone. No jeep available? Then we "hitched" with whatever vehicle was going our way. As a last resort, we marched. But it got us there.

The media appreciated our support. When applicable, we even shared any notes or information we had collected along the way for our own stories. The media was quick to share things, too. Something many of them safely packed in their grip was a bottle or two of Jim Beam or Jack Daniels. The most I had seen was six bottles. There is no better way of getting acquainted with the press than by a little socializing. We enjoyed their company and lending a helping hand. Our close relationship with the press helped maximize media coverage. Hardly a day went by without the public reading front-page stories about the First Marine Division. Meanwhile, radio stations were broadcasting daily reports about Marines in combat.

As the war accelerated, still more reporters and VIPs came to Korea. Their first stop was Tokyo, Japan. Many members of the visiting press would spend a day at the Tokyo Press Club and touch base with the United Nations Command Headquarters, which was close by. Then, acclimated to the war, the next step was a flight to Korea. After landing near Seoul, they took a press train that brought them to the First Marine Division Headquarters. It was easy to spot our PIO news tent, because there were flocks of civilian reporters hanging around. Our news center was busier than most of the three-ring-circus big tops I had seen as a kid. From *Time* magazine to the *New York Times*—and from masses of smaller-market media—they came. All the news services were there—AP, INS, Reuters, and UP. All the radio networks were there, too: ABC, CBS, and NBC. All the media, which is highly competitive, wanted their share of front page coverage. That's why the Marines PIO drew a lot of the big-name VIPs, including, Walter Cronkite, Marguerite Higgins, James A. Michener, and Edward R. Murrow. The Korean War, by the way, made Maggie Higgins, war correspondent for the *New York Herald Tribune*, famous.

It was a circus-like atmosphere to be sure. But the Marines had an experienced ringmaster to handle the big show. A reservist called to active duty, Capt. Bem Price took over the division PIO in October 1952. A former AP news reporter, he had walked in the civilian correspondents' boots. He knew about deadlines and war reporting. Bem Price knew the reporters were under pressure from their editors to scoop the other guys. So, at times, he found ways to file their stories faster by cutting military red tape. (Since Korea, with all the increased competition from cable and the Internet, the media today faces even tighter hair-trigger deadlines.)

BONDING

The media had a close relationship with the Marines. Reporters knew they would always get a story.

Besides his many administrative responsibilities, Bem Price was the first to lead the reporters to the front lines. Obviously he and his key people could not handle all the requests for them to travel to the MLR, so that was where we Combat Correspondents came in. When available, we took turns as escorts. Despite the demands from the media circus surrounding him, Price performed He seemed to thrive in the wall-to-wall chaos. Price was the right man at the right job at the right time, and it was a great break for me to serve in his command.

During this period I noticed the special bond between the media and the Marines. The media had an insatiable appetite for stories featuring the U.S. Marines. I do not say this with a bias. The facts speak for themselves. All you have to do is check the newspaper archives. Check the *New York Times*, for example. There you will find that the dominant newspaper coverage that featured the Marines, from the Inchon landing to the Chosin Reservoir battle and the defense of the Main Line of Resistance with the other UN forces.

When touring the front lines, the civilian reporters had no objection to wearing a helmet and flak jacket. It made them look like one of us. On one such journey to the Seventh Regiment with a *Newsweek* magazine reporter, I stopped the jeep and told him to "hold on." We were approaching an open stretch that we called "Sniper Valley." It was an area on the road about 1/8th of mile long where the Chinese snipers liked to practice their marksmanship. It did not happen every day. But the risk was there. So, to speed past the open target area, I gunned the jeep. We went from zero to 30 mph in five seconds. (The military jeeps were notoriously underpowered regarding speed. This changed when the Chrysler Corporation bought the name years later. Then it became "Jeep" with a capital "J.") The sniper did get off four or five rounds, missing us by twenty yards. I am sure the reporter has retold this story to his grandchildren, and maybe embellished it a little amid fading memories.

The Marines that were singled out, interviewed, and photographed by the press enjoyed their 15 minutes of fame. They knew their family and friends back home would be reading about them. The reporters were careful to spell the names correctly and made sure the hometowns matched the right state. (There are 140 towns named Springfield in the U.S.A.) Some visiting reporters doubled in duty as a photojournalist. The photojournalists were few. One that comes to mind is David Douglas Duncan. In Korea, he was on assignment with *Life* magazine. DDD was a former Marine Combat Correspondent during World War II. But if the media needed photo support, our CC photographers would help out. Same for the broadcast side. I occasionally recorded stories that CBS and the other radio networks requested from their base in Tokyo. In a way, it was doing their work for them, but we were happy to fulfill the media's special requests. It promoted the Marine Corps.

Like a wise Solomon, Bem Price reminded us: "Who cares who gets the by-line or picture credit, as long as it showcases the Marines. Besides, it's the media—the newspapers, magazines and broadcast networks—that provide the big picture." How right he was.

Bem Price's name popped up frequently in the best-selling book by Garry Cameron, *Last to Know, First to Go*, published by the United States Marine Corps Combat Correspondents Association. Cameron's book includes this excerpt about Price's stand on communications and his diplomatic skills as a Public Affairs officer:

In October 1952, Capt. Bem Price—called to active duty after covering the early days of war as an AP correspondent—took over as division Public Information Officer. The division dug in and fought the war from static positions. The South Koreans were on guard to the left of the truce corridor. On the right, on the forward slope of a high hill, was combat outpost #2 overlooking Panmunjom. Civilian correspondents and VIPs journeyed to the outpost to watch proceedings at the truce site. Although the truce corridor was an artificial situation, it still provided a source for many stories.

EMBEDDED

Two numbers I've never forgotten from boot camp days: Serial number - 1230792. Rifle number - 1654855. But please don't ask me to repeat all my general orders.

Capt. Bem Price, CO, PIO officer, was the ideal ring-master for the media circus in 1952. (Associated Press Corporate Archives, AP 21.2, Bem Price Papers)

As neutral ground, it served as a sanctuary. If a combat patrol from either side was getting the worst of a firefight, the losers could step inside the "safe" corridor and end the exchange. According to rules accepted by both sides, no one could fire into or from the truce corridor.

Munsan-ni was a railhead where the press train was located in the division zone. The Marine PIO had the responsibility of from 25 to 50 civilian correspondents. On Price's first evening in the division, he was invited to the commanding general's briefing for division staff officers and regimental commanders. Price had not yet met the general. During the briefing, the general reiterated previous orders that all officers tell the correspondents nothing and discourage them from visiting division units.

"I stood up and introduced myself, explained my background and told him bluntly that if that order stood, I might as well pack my gear and go home," Price recalled later. After thinking for a moment the general said: "Belay those last instructions." Afterward, with close cooperation by the general and Cols. Henry W. Buse and Lewis Walt, Bem Price was able to accomplish his mission.

During Bem Price's watch, many major stories emanated from the Division PIO News Center. I was personally involved with two of them. The first was on October 27, 1952 when the Seventh Regiment got hit hard on the Hook ridge up on the MLR. Sgt. Francis Grunert of Trenton, New Jersey, was captured, but was pulled to freedom three hours later by two Marines. I recorded him at the First Battalion Medical Aid Station. The story went national and Grunert was tagged "the Lucky Leatherneck." Six of his platoon buddies were killed. Then in April 1953, Capt. Price previewed a tape I had recorded with Ted Williams, the baseball Hall of Famer. He had it transcribed, then prepared news releases for the media. It went worldwide as a spot-news story. (See the chapters entitled *Lucky Leatherneck* and *Ted Williams' Close Call*.)

Edward R. Murrow, the legendary CBS newscaster, was among the many famous VIPs visiting the First Marine Division in Korea. Here's an excerpt about his visit from *Last to Know, First to Go*, by Garry Cameron:

VIP

Edward R. Murrow was one of the CBS broadcasters to visit Marines in Korea.

Shortly before Christmas, 1953, the venerable Edward R. Murrow arrived in Korea to film what would be his last Christmas show of its kind. To the chagrin of the Eighth Army PIO, Murrow declared that he would personally cover the Marines and send his fellow CBS correspondents to cover the Army. And no, he didn't want or need an Eighth Army escort.

"Hell, if there's any kind of action out here after the cease-fire, I figure the Marines will lead me to it," he told his Marine PIO escort.

Arriving in a jeep followed by a huge Army truck loaded with his elaborate 35mm tripod cameras, sound equipment, his cameraman and sound technician—plus a case of his favorite bourbon he later shared with some of the line Marines he covered—Murrow was escorted to the forward-most front line overlooking the DMZ. There he interviewed Marines manning the foxhole outposts atop a hill, including Navy Cross holder, Capt. Bill Bates.

Thanks to George Clooney, the younger generation will learn more about Edward R. Murrow. Clooney both starred in and directed the film, *Good Night, and Good Luck*. It is about Murrow's weekly CBS-TV series, *See It Now*, which I and millions of others enjoyed watching in the 1950s. David Strathairn starred as Murrow.

Some people thought that the media "favored" the Marine Corps in its Korean War coverage. My brother, Ken, who had served in the Army during World War II, thought so. He contended that the Eighth Army, which had three times the troops as the Marines, should have had the lion's share of coverage. I tried to explain that it doesn't work that way. The civilian reporters could write about any military group they wished. But, as pointed out earlier, the Marines were the draw as they had some of the roughest assignments: the successful Inchon landing, the Chosin Reservoir battle, and the static MLR war of 1952–53, during which the Marines were pitted against the skilled Chinese fighters. Did the media favor the Marines? No way. But there was a "special bond" between them. Among all of the UN forces' sectors—including the U.S. Eighth Army—the Marines had what the media thrives on: front-page potential.

Here is a sample of the news that the media filed from Korea:

1st Marine Div Awarded

ROK President's Citation

WITH U.S. 1ST MARINE DIV - (UP) - Mar. 25, 1953 -

The "outnumbered but never outfought" First Marine Division today was awarded the Korean presidential citation.

This was the first unit citation by a foreign government to a Marine outfit since World War I when the 2d Marine Brigade was awarded the *croix de guerre* by the French government.

PRESIDENT SYNGMAN RHEE cited the division for its year long defense of the Seoul invasion route in which "Marines won everlasting glory at Bunker Hill."

In addition, the Leathernecks were cited for their fight against the initial attack by the Chinese Communists at Chosin reservoir in the winter of 1950 and for their counterattack in April 1951.

"THIS COUNTERATTACK came," said the citation, "when other Republic of Korea forces were heavily pressed and fighting for their survival. The timely offensive by this division gave heart to the peoples of Korea."

The presentation of the award was made by Admiral Shohm Woon II, Korean chief of naval operations, to Maj. Gen. E. A. Pollock, commanding general of the First Marine Division in a formal ceremony today.

PRESIDENT RHEE noted in the citation that "the First Marine Division earned three American Presidential Unit Citations while participating in amphibious operations in the Asiatic Pacific theater."

Since the beginning of the Korean War, the unit has earned nine battle stars on its Korean ribbon and an American Presidential Unit Citation for its part in the Inchon landing in September, 1950.

South Korean President, Syngman Rhee (white suit), reviews troops at the 1st Marine Division in August 1952. Accompanying him is Maj. Gen. E. A. Pollack, CO of the division. (Author's Collection)

Here is another story featuring the Marines, this one from both the UP and INS on March 28, 1953:

Besides Bunker Hill, Hook, Reno, Siberia and Vegas, there were the "girls." These included Ava, Dagmar, Esther, Ginger, Ingrid, and Marilyn. The Marines had fun naming their outposts.

Marines Recapture Vegas Hill

SEOUL, MAR. 28, (UP) American Marines recaptured shell-pocked Vegas Hill this afternoon to win round four of a see-saw battle for the United Nations outposts blocking the invasion route to Seoul.

* * *

SEOUL, MAR. 28 (INS) Stubborn Chinese infantrymen clung to a bitterly disputed western front outpost today, standing up to a withering Allied air and artillery barrage and turning back four Marine counterattacks in the see-saw contest for the position.

The Chinese, who captured Outposts Vegas and Reno near Bunker hill Thursday night, hung on grimly to both positions today, and a pocket of Red soldiers successfully defended Vegas against night-long Marine efforts to retake it.

THE MARINES charged up the slopes of Vegas last night and initially reported they secured the position. But a Chinese pocket held firmly to the north slope of the hill and laid down a curtain of fire that made the crest too hot for the leathernecks to hold.

At last reports, Marines were crouching in their foxholes at the base of Vegas as artillery pounded the Communists on the north slope. The last attack against the Chinese position on the north slope was made at 9:30 this morning.

The Marines were subjected to the heaviest Communist artillery bombardment since last October Thursday night and yesterday. The Eighth Army reported Communist gunners fired almost 41,000 shells into

Allied positions during the 24-hour period ending at 6 p.m. yesterday and concentrated almost 36,000 of these shells in the Marine defenses.

ALLIED TANKS and big guns dueled with Chinese artillerymen in the Old Baldy sector, where a Communist assault captured the mountain above one of the roads to Seoul from American and Colombian troops of the Seventh Division.

America's press people did their homework before they came to Korea. Most of them could have been history professors. While chatting with one of the reporters from the *Chicago Tribune*—we were jeeping to the front lines—he talked about China. He pointed out that the same Communist Chinese soldiers that were there in Korea had been fighting Generalissimo Chiang Kai-shek's National troops for decades. Interestingly, he personally remembered when the two China-enemies were united against the Japanese during their invasion into China. Then, after Japan's defeat in 1945, for which America was responsible, the two archrivals resumed their private war. Each wanted to rule mainland China. Finally in 1949, the Communists prevailed. They conquered China. (The United States had been supporting the loser, Chiang Kai-shek.) The Communists literally pushed Chiang Kai-shek and his Nationalists out of China and onto Taiwan. Now they were coming after America.

The Chicago reporter was convinced that had the United Nations forces stopped at the 38th parallel in the fall of 1950—and not continued to route the North Korean Army toward Manchuria—the Chinese may not have entered the war. We were warned about it. The Chinese sent messages several times, saying that to cross north of the 38th Parallel would be a violation of the Korean treaty. (Just as the North Korean People's Army violated the same treaty in June of 1950 by invading Seoul.) Be that as it may, the Communist Chinese, in November–December of 1950, started sneaking troops over the Manchurian border. Pretty soon we spotted them. But it was too late. Their numbers surged to a "Red Tide." In all, 780,000 troops joined their North Korean allies. With them they brought battlefield skills and equipment that they had used against the Chinese Nationalists. They were ready to take on the United Nations forces, including the U.S. Eighth Army and First Marine Division.

During my tour in Korea in 1952–1953, the war became a static one. The Marines faced the Chinese while much of the Eighth Army and other UN forces were in the North Korean Army's sector. The Chinese despised the Marines, and even put a bounty on them. You did not want to be a POW (prisoner of war) in the hands of the Communist Chinese.

Reporters and war correspondents came from all over the world to cover the Korean War. They were anxious to get to the front lines. They knew that nothing sold newspapers like war. Their editors and publishers had reminded them that speed is everything. "Get the story before competition beats you to it," they were urged.

The Civilian Press Corps was made up mostly of the following groups during the Korean War:

- **News Services of Associated Press, INS, Reuters, and UP.** Their reporters came to Korea to feed their media subscribers the war news. Virtually all newspapers and radio and television stations subscribed to at least one of the wire services. The news came over teletype machines from all over the world to the media's newsrooms. The number of bells ringing denoted the importance of any incoming story. (Note: INS later merged with UP and became UPI.)

- **Newspapers**. Many editors sent their top reporters to cover the Korean War. The *New York Times, Washington Post, Wall Street Journal, Chicago Tribune,* and even some small-market papers sent reporters. Freelancers came too, such as James Michener, author of *South Pacific*.

- **Magazines**. Favorite magazines of the day were represented, including: *Time, Look, Newsweek,* and *U.S. News and World Report. Life* sent David Douglas Duncan to shoot photos.

- **Radio and Television**. The Korean War was primarily a "radio war," as television was still in its infancy. The radio networks of ABC, CBS, and NBC filed most of their newscasts from Tokyo. The Marine Radio Correspondents supplied the networks with spot news stories. A few network people visited the war zone, including CBS's Walter Cronkite and Edward R. Murrow.

- **Movie Newsreels**. *Fox Movietone News* was experienced in covering wars and disasters. They had excellent cameramen who felt right at home on the "firing line" of the Korean War. Their role was important, since many Americans depended on

73

newsreels for their "visual" source of news. Sadly, years later, with television gaining viewers, this medium died out. Today's younger generation missed out on a great way to view the world.

Getting to Korea to cover the war was not easy, especially for the eastern media. One of the reporters from the *New York Times* explained:

> The first leg of the trip was from New York City to Los Angeles. That took hours. Then LA to Honolulu, Hawaii. That part seemed like days. From there we flew in to Tokyo, Japan. That jaunt—again, over water—took forever. We landed. I spent several days at the Tokyo Press Club and got prepped for my assignment. A rickshaw ride away was the United Nations Command Headquarters. I was able to get a good war overview from the UN public relations people. Then, on a plane again. From Tokyo to Seoul, Korea. From Seoul I rode the press train to the First Marine Division. Then a jarring jeep ride to the firing line. Whew! It was like fighting a war to get to the war.

The media did not have to come to Korea for war news. They could have stayed home and gotten the news off the "ticker" in their newsroom. Or they could opt for the comfortable surroundings in Tokyo, Japan. Besides a modern press club, not far away in Tokyo was the United Nations Command News Center. Yet the media, true to the profession, wanted a guardian or watchdog role for their readers and listeners. Dedicated editors and publishers sent their best reporters to Korea for eyewitness reports.

For example, CBS's Walter Cronkite reported directly from Korea on radio. James A. Michener, on the print side, the author of *South Pacific*, did some freelance reporting for various newspapers. A fellow combat correspondent, Cpl. Jack Paxton, escorted Mr. Michener in the Marine's Fifth Battalion area for two days in 1951. Later, in the U.S. Eighth Army sector, Michener wrote an article that inspired another best seller, *Bridges of ToKoRi*. The story told of a downed U.S. Navy VF-194 jet from the Valley Forge Aircraft Carrier. Later, the

Marguerite Higgins, New York Herald Tribune, *center, Carl Mydans*, Life *magazine, behind her (no camera), and colleagues by the Han River in 1950. They were the first reporters to cover the Korean War. (Photo Courtesy Doubleday and Company)*

movie, starring William Holden, Fredric March, and Mickey Rooney, was produced.

WAR MEMOIRS

Jack Paxton, former CC, escorted James A. Michener to the front lines in 1951.

A side note. After his Marine tour of duty, Jack Paxton was in management with GTE. He met James Michener again at a National Governors' Conference in Austin, Texas in 1985. They had a good visit about their first meeting, and rehashed the media's role in the War. The famous author, who served as a Navy officer in World War II, felt right at home with the Marines. He treated Jack Paxton like an old, lost buddy.

Press people knew how to dress for war. The men wore khaki pants and shirts with open collars. Most had army-type jackets and wore heavy-duty boots. Each sported a picture ID badge clipped to their shirt pocket or belt. Some of the flashier dressers came with an aviator's jacket. Headcover? Some wore military fatigue caps. A few preferred a tattered baseball cap with their team's logo. (Most were New York Yankee fans. Second choice was the Chicago White Sox.) What about the women? They dressed about the same as their male counterparts. It was often hard to tell the gals from the guys. MSgt. H.B. Wells, one of our combat photographers, astutely observed that if you looked for "stuffed" shirt pockets, it became easier to tell them apart. H.B. always had a keen eye. Maybe that is why he was a photographer.

Despite the many inconveniences—cold water, cold chow and cold winters—dozens of journalists wanted the Korean War assignment. And like Walter Cronkite, James Michener, and Edward R. Murrow, many camped out at the Marine's PIO headquarters. There were no private suites. Early arrivals were assigned a cot. Latecomers got a sleeping bag—on the deck. No gourmet chow, either, but the old-timers knew how to make things a little better. They brought a bottle. Or two. Usually Jim Beam. They always shared. Meanwhile, over at U.S. Eighth Army PIO, the housing, ambiance, chow, etc., was closer to five-star luxury living. The reporters favored covering the Marines because, as Marguerite Higgins, a *New York Herald Tribune* reporter, said, there was less red tape and stuffiness, compared to the Army. She earlier had received a "cold" welcome from them, and never forgot it.

ROUGHING IT

Reporters were good sports. They accepted the less-than-luxurious conditions.

Speaking of Miss Higgins, I wish I could have been there to see her arrival in Korea. It was the third day of the war, June 27, 1950. Seoul was under siege by the North Korean Army. American advisors were ordered out of Seoul. They were waiting for their rescue plane at Kimpo Airfield, close to Seoul. A huge C-54 aircraft was circling the field.

The American advisors in Korea could hardly wait to board that "last plane out of Seoul." The plane finally landed. Then its cargo door opened. There were four reporters waiting by the hatch. First off was Marguerite Higgins of the *New York Herald Tribune*, who made a big splash as a woman war correspondent. Joining her—no one remembers the exact sequence—were fellow reporters Keyes Beech of the *Chicago Daily News*, Burton Crane of the *New York Times*, and Frank Gibney with *Time* magazine.

An irony! As some Americans were leaving besieged Seoul, reporters were just arriving to launch the biggest media event of the year. It was a media circus that would play until July 1953.

GUTSY LADY

Marguerite Higgins stood her ground. She refused to leave even when Gen. MacArthur ordered her out of Korea.

Miss Higgins ran into a buzz saw of discrimination almost from the minute she stepped on Korean soil. General MacArthur told her, "No women reporters here." But later he rescinded the order. Five years earlier than Rosa Parks, the African-American seamstress from Montgomery, Alabama, who would defy racial discrimination on a bus, Higgins stood her ground in Korea against gender discrimination. She helped advance her cause of equal access for female war correspondents. Both she and Rosa Parks became national heroes.

A smart journalist, Miss Higgins kept copious notes and rushed them into one of the first books on the Korean War, *War in Korea, The Report of a Woman Combat Correspondent*. It was published in 1951. Out of print and scarce, I had to borrow a copy from the University of Minnesota library to reread it. An avalanche of books on the "forgotten war" were to follow, but "Maggie" Higgins could proudly claim: "Mine was first!" And it sold. Americans were hungry for information about Korea.

I have carefully chosen this excerpt from her book that shows her daring. She is on a landing craft with the 5th Marines in September 1950 headed toward "Red Beach" during the infamous Inchon landing. She wanted to produce an eyewitness report of how Marines fought wars:

―――――――――――

"Wave Number Five," someone shouted, and we threaded our way through the confusion on deck to our prearranged position. Our wave commander, Lieutenant R.J. Shening, yelled at us to be careful climbing down the cargo nets into our craft. The cargo nets were made of huge, rough ropes. The trick was to hang onto the big knots with all your strength while you groped with your feet for the swaying rungs below.

I dropped last into the boat, which was now packed with thirty-eight heavily laden Marines, ponchos on their backs and rifles on their shoulders. As we shoved away from the transport, sheets of spray were flung back upon us by the wind.

We must have circled almost an hour, picking up the rest of the craft in Wave Number Five. I was thoroughly keyed up, but the Marines around me were elaborately calm. Two of them played gin rummy on the wooden cover over the engine. They only stopped when the lurching of the boat scattered their cards all over the wet planks.

Then it was H hour. The first wave pulled out of the circle and headed for the beach. We all stared fixedly at the shore—about two thousand yards away—and tried to guess, from the expressions on the faces of the seamen returning from the beach in their empty boats, what it had been like.

The control ship signaled that it was our turn.

"Here we go—keep your heads down," shouted Lieutenant Shening.

As we rushed toward the sea wall an amber-colored star shell burst above the beach. It meant that our first objective, the cemetery, had been taken. But be-

TOO EFFICIENT

After Korea I was stationed at Glenview Naval Air Station in Glenview, Illinois. I saw a sailor on the gate. Not a Marine. Here's why: The week before, the admiral had been ordered to halt and show ID. Instead of stopping, the CO's vehicle rolled through without following orders. The young Marine guard fired his .45 in the air. The next day the Navy took over gate duty.

fore we could even begin to relax, brightly colored tracer bullets cut across our bow and across the open top of our boat. I heard the authoritative rattle of machine guns. Somehow the enemy had survived the terrible pounding they'd been getting. Then our boat smashed into a dip in the sea wall. With the deadly crisscross of bullets whining above them, the Marines involuntarily continued to crouch low in the boat.

"Come on, you big, brave Marines—let's get the hell out of here," yelled Lieutenant Shening, emphasizing his words with good, hard shoves.

A warning burst, probably a grenade, forced us all down, and we snaked along on our stomachs over the boulders to a sort of curve below the top of the dip. It gave us a cover of sorts from the tracer bullets, and we three newsmen and most of the Marines flattened out and waited there. As we waited, wave after wave of Marines hit the beach, and soon there must have been sixty or more of us lying on our bellies in the small dip.

One Marine ventured over the ridge, but he jumped back so hurriedly that he stamped one foot hard onto my bottom. This fortunately has considerable padding, but it did hurt. He removed his foot hastily and apologized in a tone that indicated his amazement that he had been walking on a woman. I think he was the only Marine who recognized me as a woman—my helmet and overcoat were good camouflage.

Maggie Higgins' stories about the Inchon landing scored with her readers. A good judge of people and organizations, she explained how the U.S. Army and the U.S. Marine Corps treated reporters differently:

The Marine, as an individual, is usually extremely proud of his organization. He welcomes correspondents because they are there to tell the rest of the world about the job he is doing. Also, since they are a smaller organization than the Army, the Marines are less stuffy and less involved in red tape. It is easier for them to help you out.

The military and media were unified in their efforts to report the news during the Korean War. Not so in the Iraqi war. The U.S. military has launched its own service in Iraq and Afghanistan to send military video, text, and photos directly to the Internet or news outlets. The $6.3 million project is one of the largest military public affairs projects in recent memory, and it is intended to allow small media outlets in the United States and elsewhere to bypass what the Pentagon views as an increasingly combative press corps. Interestingly, FOX Cable News has pointed out this same media bias regarding coverage of the Iraqi war. (All bad news; no good news.)

U.S. officials have complained that Iraq-based media focus on catastrophic events such as car bombs and soldiers' deaths, while giving short shrift to U.S. rebuilding efforts. The project, called Digital Video and Imagery Distribution System (DVIDS), will also give the Pentagon more control of the coverage when calamities do happen. Much of the effort is aimed at packaging and shipping locally focused stories to small- and medium-sized newspapers and television stations.

Most small U.S. media outlets cannot afford to send a reporter to Iraq to cover a local military unit. Since

MILITARY-MEDIA

The military-press relationship has changed. They were unified in their efforts in Korea. In Iraq, some of the media has ignored the rebuilding efforts and focused on negative events. Thus the U.S. officials have started Digital Video and Imagery Distribution System (DVIDS). This will assure smaller markets of seeing news of their National Guard unit doing good work in Iraq.

HARVARD STUDY?

Korea's media circus would make a classic case-study for the Harvard Business School. It provides an intriguing insight into the unified media-military position at the Marines' PIO news center. It would also make a stark contrast with the military-press relationship of today.

the ongoing troop rotation involves several National Guard and Reserve units from communities across the United States, some small media outlets might never get news of their neighbors' work in Iraq. Not taking anything away from this effort to provide a better balance of news in Iraq, the Marines produced hometown radio tapes ("Joe Blow" interviews) for these same small markets during the Korean war. The project was highly successful. (See the *Combat Correspondents* chapter.)

The media circus in Korea would make a classic case-study for the Harvard Business School. It was the biggest international media event in the 1950s. For me, it meant working with some real pros in the Marines' Combat Correspondent program, and building a long-term relationship with the media. It also held a special meaning for Marguerite Higgins. As a result of her role in the "media circus," Ms. Higgins was the first woman to win a Pulitzer Prize. In memoriam—she died in 1966—she was featured on a postage stamp in 2002, recognizing women in journalism. It is fitting that Maggie Higgins is interred at Arlington National Cemetery, close to many of the same Marines she reported on during the Korean War.

Here are some key players that covered the Korean War, which became one of the biggest media events in the 1950's:

Participants: America's First Media Circus

REPORTERS

Keyes Beech – *Chicago Daily News*
Burton Crane – *New York Times*

Walter Cronkite – CBS

David Douglas Duncan – *Life*

Frank Gibney – *Time*

Marguerite Higgins – *New York Herald Tribune*

James A. Mitchener – Freelance reporter

Edward R. Murrow – CBS

Carl Mydans – *Life*

Bem Price – Associated Press (later served as Marine PIO officer)

NEWSPAPERS

Chicago Daily News
Chicago Tribune
New York Herald Tribune
New York Times
Philadelphia Enquirer
Wall Street Journal
Washington Post
(and many more major and small market papers)

MAGAZINES

Life
Look
Newsweek
Time
U.S. News and World Report

NEWS SERVICES

AP – (Associated Press)
INS – (International News Service)
Reuters
UP (United Press)

Mission-bound is Capt. Ted Williams, Panther jet pilot, based at VMF-311 Squadron, First Marine Air Wing, Pusan, Korea, April 1953. (Marine Corps Photo)

6

TED WILLIAMS' CLOSE CALL

I crossed paths several times with Ted Williams, the baseball Hall of Famer. The first occasion was at Nicollet Park in Minneapolis when I was just a kid. Williams was in the minor leagues with the Minneapolis Millers, a Boston Red Sox farm team. Wow! Could he slam home runs! He was a tall, lanky 20-year-old and a natural-born hitter. He batted left, threw right-handed and played right field. I was eight years old and a devoted fan of his. You can imagine my surprise when he was introduced to me and the whole Knot Hole Gang sitting in the right-field bleachers. For kids with no pocket money, the Millers started a club for us and let us in free on Saturdays. Williams chatted with us just before a game with the Toledo Mud Hens. We won. It would be 15 years before we met again. It was Korea in 1953. Now we were both in the Marines. He was Capt. Ted Williams, jet pilot. I was a sergeant and a radio correspondent.

Williams, a Marine reserve officer, was 31 years old when the Korean War started on June 25, 1950. He had been a Marine pilot in World War II. They would not interrupt his baseball career twice, would they? He did not have many more times at bat. Williams did not realize how badly the military needed pilots. He went on active duty on May 1, 1952. Now he was 33. He trained as a jet fighter pilot at Cherry Point, North Carolina. Shortly after arriving in Korea in February 1953, he was making news on the battlefield, a long ways from Boston's Fenway Park baseball stadium. During his third combat mission, on February 16, 1953, his F9 Panther jet was hit by enemy ground fire after destroying troop installations in North Korea. Then, with his plane on fire, a dead radio, few functioning gauges, and only one wheel, he coaxed in his plane. It crashed. Capt. Williams, used to bumps and bruises on the ball field, shook off the incident and was in the lineup to fly the next

GOOD NEWS. BAD NEWS.

Marines activate Ted Williams. Baseball fans lose a slugger.

day. More than a close call, he had avoided death by only the slimmest of margins. His fellow flyers in the VMF-311 Squadron, the legendary Pohang-by-the-Sea stationed in Pusan, South Korea, kidded Williams that he was trying to upstage John Wayne.

I learned all of this first-hand from Capt. Ted Williams during a radio interview with him that nearly never took place. It was April 13, 1953, and I was busy networking with my contacts for some radio stories. I called Bob Larson, a Minnesota guy, Yeoman Third Class, United States Navy, with the VMF-311 Squadron at Pusan. This was part of the First Marine Air Wing. He was in administration and knew everything that was going on. I inquired about Marine jet pilots. "Any news?" I asked him by phone from our Public Information Office (PIO) tent at division headquarters. He told me he was not supposed to tell me, but a very famous Marine jet flyer with the initials of T.W. was resting on a hospital ship. Our Minnesota ties helped me get the full information. Larson was one Navy man that liked Marines. I thanked him for the lead and told myself to send him a note of appreciation. As anyone in journalism will tell you, news contacts are invaluable.

I got ready my tape recorder, microphone, and several boxes of 3M reel-to-reel audio tape. I would not need to lug the portable generator and gas can this time, because there would be power on the hospital ship. I stopped at the helicopter pad and lined up a flight to the ship. Next, I shared my plans with MSgt. Joe Hensley. He was my boss and the NCO in charge of Radio Correspondents. He immediately liked the idea of a radio story with Ted Williams, but did not think it was possible. "Why not?" I asked.

"Captain Williams hasn't been chummy with press since he landed in Korea," Joe said.

TED WON'T TALK

After being recalled, Capt. Ted Williams avoided the media, until a young radio correspondent hit his hot button.

"But isn't that just the case with the civilian press corps? He's not mad at Marine Correspondents, is he?" I inquired.

"No, not you personally. But he's still miffed—pissed would be a better word—for being called back to active duty."

"But...," I half interrupted, "...he was in the reserves, wasn't he? There's always a chance you'll be activated."

"He was playing his best baseball. He's 34 years old. He doesn't have many years left to bat. And he served in World War II. How would you feel about having your baseball career interrupted—a second time—and have to climb in a jet plane at that age? And have to fly combat missions. Hell, he's already been shot down once," Hensley pointed out.

I understood what Joe was talking about. I would be pissed off, too. "So, I have my work cut out for me, don't I?" The master sergeant did not have to answer that question. I still had about 30 minutes before a chopper would drop me at Pusan, close to the hospital ship. Knowing Hensley was an encyclopedia of information, I asked for some background on Ted Williams. Like a huge computer, he spit it out.

"Ted Williams was born and raised in Marine Corps country, San Diego, California, in 1918. He excelled in everything he pursued. In baseball he was considered to be one of the greatest hitters of all time. In 1941 he hit .406. He's the most consistent hitter around. Never goes below .300. He was hitting .400 last year when he had to leave baseball and go back in the Marines. How does he do it? Combining keen vision with quick wrists and a scientific approach to hitting, that's how. He's set numerous batting records. His accomplishments include a .406 season in 1941, two Triple Crowns, two MVP's and six American League batting championships. And so far, 324 home runs. And I nearly forgot, sergeant. He bats left, throws right, is six-foot-three and weighs a little over 200 pounds. And oh, wears number nine for the Boston Red Sox."

"Whew!!! How do you know all this?" I asked the statistical wizard.

"Cuz I'm a Ted Williams fan, " he responded.

And so was I, like millions of other baseball fans. I told Joe I used to watch Williams play for the Minneapolis Millers, a Triple-A farm team for the Red Sox. I was just a kid. That was 1938. Ted Williams was one of the best players the Millers ever had. Now, I hoped, I was going to conduct a radio interview with him.

The helicopter took less than an hour, flying low, to arrive in Pusan. And just off the coast, maybe two or three hundred yards, in the Korea Strait, sat the USS *Haven*, a Navy hospital ship serving the United Nations Forces. I boarded a dinghy and in about 10 minutes I was on board. It took a while to find the administrator's office and get a pass to go see Williams, my sports hero. He was convalescing for a touch of

As a Minneapolis Miller at Nicollet Park in 1938, Ted Williams won the American Association Triple Crown, batting .336 with 43 homers. Fifteen years later in Korea, the author told Williams about seeing him play in Minneapolis and scored an interview with the jet pilot. (Minnesota Historical Society)

Winners of all kinds have one common trait—consistency. Ted Williams had the ability to hit .300 year after year. In 1941 he hit .401.

pneumonia, but he had many problems resulting from cold weather. The Navy Corpsman took me to the area where Capt. Williams was resting, a small social hall where the service men could stretch their legs and relax. It even had a piano. Capt. Williams was dressed in a blue hospital robe. He was cordial when I was introduced to him, but stern in his answer when I told him what I was on board for. Joe Hensley was right. He was reluctant to talk to the press. I mentioned that the radio interview was for the *Marine Corps Show*, which was broadcast on NBC Saturday nights and aired nationwide. His answer was a firm, "No!" Sensing a good story, I searched for his "hot button." Some connection to get the baseball legend to change his mind. My mind wandered back to that summer when I saw him play at Nicollet Park in Minneapolis.

"Capt. Williams, I used to watch you play for the Minneapolis Millers," I opened.

His mood changed a little. "You did? What year did you see me with the Millers?"

"It would have been in 1938, because you went to the Red Sox in 1939," I answered.

"What position did I play?" he returned.

He nearly had me. I had to quickly recall the outfield. I knew it was left field for most of his years with the Red Sox. "Right field?" I tried.

"What was the name of the ball park?" he asked, almost hoping I would not know.

That was easy. Everyone in Minneapolis knew about Nicollet Park at Lake and Nicollet Avenue. I told him. And he nodded to confirm that I was right.

"What was my number?" he quizzed again.

That was a tough one. Then I remembered that Joe Hensley had mentioned Williams wore number nine with the Red Sox. It probably was the same with the Millers. But wait, was this a trap? Maybe he wore a different number with his minor league teams. Then it hit me. There he was in right field. I was a kid again in the bleachers. I could see Ted Williams plain as day. "Was it 19?" I cautiously asked.

"Okay, wise guy. Last question. How many homers did I hit in 1938?"

This guy could really play hard ball. Fortunately, even as a kid, I was pretty good with baseball stats. "About 40 homers?" I volunteered.

"Forty three," he corrected me. Then he smiled his famous Ted Williams smile, and laughed. He agreed to do the radio broadcast and he hit a grand slam of an interview. He would not let me go. He reminisced about the Minneapolis Millers and everything else for another hour. Oh, how he missed baseball.

I did not realize how big the story was until I got back to the PIO Radio headquarters at the First Marine Division. Waiting for me was Joe Hensley and Bem Price, Commanding Officer, PIO. They played the tape twice and were excited about the story. It meant that Ted Williams had broken his press silence. Most

The USS Haven, *a United Nations hospital ship off the eastern coast of Korea and site of the radio interview with Ted Williams. (Author's Collection)*

importantly, the public would get news about the Marines' most famous sports figure in Korea.

"This one goes on the wire," ordered Capt. Price. A former Associated Press writer and a Marine reservist, he knew a page-one story when he heard one. He had my radio tape transcribed and prepared as a press release for all media. The story hit the newspapers the next day, and was picked up by all the radio networks. Capt. Ted Williams had been under the impression the story was only for the *Marine Corps Show*, but I had no control over how the story would be used. It went worldwide. Years later, I learned he was pleased that his interview from the USS *Haven* received all the extra media coverage. This made me feel good.

Below is my interview with Ted Williams, the Boston Red Sox superstar and Marine Corps jet pilot:

HILL: This is Marine Radio Correspondent, Dick Hill, with the First Marine Division in Korea. We're located aboard the United States Naval Hospital Ship, the USS *Haven*, somewhere off the coast of South Korea where our microphone is set up to bring you an interview with a Marine who is familiar to all the sports world. He is Captain Ted Williams, presently serving with the First Marine Air Wing here in Korea. And first off, Captain, I want to say that it's a real pleasure to be able to talk to you and see you up and about. What exactly brought you here to the USS *Haven*, hospital ship?

WILLIAMS: Well, Dick, I came down with pneumonia of all things about two weeks ago and I was sent out here to the *Haven* for some recuperating. And I must say that I'm certainly getting wonderful treatment.

HILL: How long have you been in Korea?

WILLIAMS: Well, I left the States January 28th and that figures out to be about six or seven weeks, I guess.

HILL: I understand that you're flying a jet plane here in Korea. A F-9 Panther jet?

WILLIAMS: That's right. I'm stationed down in the southeastern part of Korea with the First Marine Air Wing. We're flying interdiction hops mostly. I was above the bomb line destroying supplies and troop installations.

HILL: What's this about a narrow escape that you had not too long ago?

WILLIAMS: Well, I certainly did have one. It was on my third mission and I got hit up there and I caught on fire and lost a lot of the facilities on the plane and was very fortunate in coming back—being able to come back to one of our bases in southern Korea. I made a crash landing and had a pretty scary experience.

HILL: I bet it was. Captain, were you injured in any way?

WILLIAMS: Not a bit. I'm in good shape.

HILL: And speaking about thrilling experiences, Captain Williams, and getting away from the war here in Korea, could you tell the listeners back home about your most thrilling baseball experience?

WILLIAMS: Well, Dick, that is an easy one for me. I forever said that the most thrilling experience I ever had in baseball was the home run I hit in 1941 in the All-Star game in Detroit against the National League

FREQUENT FLYER

Williams had 39 missions with the First Marine Air Wing that supplied air support for ground troops.

in which we won in the ninth inning. There were two away, and we were two runs behind. I hit a home run and the American League won the All-Star game.

HILL: What about the baseball season this year. Are you keeping up on that?

WILLIAMS: Well, certainly I'm keeping up on it the best way I can through the *Stars and Stripes* and the only thing I can tell you is what I read in the papers. It's the only way I voice an opinion. But to me it looks awfully much like the Yankees are going to be unbeatable in the American League. They've strengthened their pitching staff through the coming back of Whitey Ford who I've hit against and who I know is a real outstanding young pitcher. Even though their first-line pitchers are getting a little older, I don't think it will make too much difference. They were outstanding last year and have been for the last several. There's no reason they won't be outstanding again. The New York Yankees have a well balanced club. And to me, it's the only club I can see in the American League. In the National League I think there'll be a fight over there for first honors. But I think that the Brooklyn Dodgers are the club to beat over there.

HILL: What about your plans for the future? Are they pretty well thought out?

WILLIAMS: Well, I don't know. I have a tour of duty to perform over here before I think too much about what I'm going to do when I get out. However, I'm supposed to get out sometime in September or October. And one of my first thoughts will be to get back to Florida. I'm in business down there and I'd have to look at things and see whether or not I'm going to play baseball again. It all depends how I feel. If I feel like I could do my club any good, and if Mr. Yawkey, the Red Sox president, wants me to come back, why I might try.

Ted Williams, and most of the military, relied on Stars and Stripes *for baseball news and standings.*

HILL: Captain Ted Williams, it's been a real pleasure talking to you. And I want to wish you the best of luck during the rest of your stay here in Korea. This is Marine Radio Correspondent Sgt. Dick Hill saying that you've just heard an interview with Captain Ted Williams, presently on board the USS *Haven*, a United States Naval Hospital Ship somewhere off the coast of South Korea. We return you now to the *Marine Corps Show* in Hollywood, California.

As an officer and a gentleman, Ted Williams underplayed his combat experiences. He soft-pedaled his jet crash story, but others did not. It seemed like everyone stationed in Korea "eyewitnessed" the crash. By talking to many of the men in the First Marine Air Wing—both Marine and Navy personnel—and with Captain Williams himself, here is the story I learned:

Ted Williams, with his baseball career postponed the second time, arrived in Korea on February 4, 1953. Assigned to the First Marine Air Wing, he was with the VMF-311 Squadron. There were 32 members, including John Glenn, the commanding officer. (Glenn later became a famous astronaut and U.S. Senator.) With only two missions completed, Ted Williams nearly became a casualty when he was one of the 200 flyers in a huge air mission aimed at Kyomipo, 15 miles south of the North Korean capital of Pyongyang.

Flying his F9 Panther jet, Williams was coming in low over his target when a troop encampment blasted his plane with small arms fire. Completing his run, he tried to pull up. Every warning light in the cockpit lit up and the plane started vibrating. The stick was

JOHN GLENN

Before making history as an astronaut, John Glenn was Ted Williams' CO in the VMF-311 Squadron. They became close friends. Glenn was the first American to circle the globe. Later, he was a U.S. Senator from Ohio.

Capt. Ted Williams, former Boston Red Sox slugger, is presented the Air Medal and two Gold Stars in lieu of the second and third Air Medals by Lt. Col. Bernard McShane, CO, Panther Jet Squadron, June 24, 1953. (Marine Corps Photo/Cpl. Gerald Harrington)

shaking, and he knew he had sprung a leak in the hydraulic system. The landing gear came down and the plane was hard to control. Williams got the landing gear up and started climbing. He got on the radio but it was dead. Another pilot pulled close and tried to signal Williams to bail out. Williams declined because he did not know his plane was on fire. He climbed upward and then turned his jet toward the nearest American base. His flaps were frozen and he was unable to lower the landing gear. Instinct told Williams he should eject, but he was afraid if he ejected his kneecaps would hit against the cockpit, so he stayed with the crippled plane. A companion aircraft, piloted by Lt. Larry Hawkins, led Williams back to the field and radioed ahead that Williams was in trouble.

By now the field was in sight and Williams was trying to land when an explosion rocked the craft. A wheel door had blown off. Smoke was pouring from the brake ports. Below him the residents of a small Korean village on the outskirts of the field scattered. They had seen troubled jets before. Williams' plane was a mass of fire and smoke. Unable to check his air speed, he came in "hot" at 225 miles per hour, almost twice the recommended speed for a safe landing. He dropped the emergency wheel latch, but only one dropped into position. He hit the air strip level, but he had no way to slow the plane. As ground witnesses report, the plane settled on its belly with sparks, fire, and smoke trailing after it. The jet screamed down the field out of control for more than a mile. It shed strips of metal and was on the verge of exploding. Several

THE QUIET MAN

Ted Williams avoided the media. I was proud to score the first interview with him in Korea on the USS Haven *hospital ship where he shared his war and baseball experiences.*

times the plane nearly hit the emergency fire trucks waiting for the inevitable blowup.

"THERE GOES TED!"

Some of the riflemen swore that they knew Ted Williams' jet, and would bet their buddies that it was "Ted" up there supplying air support. (Marines would bet on anything.)

Finally, at the edge of the runway, the plane groaned to a stop. Williams immediately popped the canopy. The plane was aflame. He dove headfirst to the tarmac and was grabbed by two Marine flight crewmen and was hustled away. Would he ever fly again? Were his jet days over? How could he ever make up for the loss of a million-dollar piece of government property? All these questions raced through Ted Williams' mind. Then, angry both at himself and the close call, he removed his helmet and threw it to the ground, just like he did in baseball games after a really bad call. Later, coming back to look at the damaged plane, he saw a blackened hulk. The jet was completely destroyed. Ted Williams had avoided death by the narrowest of margins. Yet the next day, like a loyal Marine, he was back in the sky.

Ted Williams became an even bigger hero of mine after the radio interview on the USS *Haven*. He had invited me to visit him at Fenway Park in Boston—providing he returned to baseball, which he did. He was soon discharged from the hospital ship and returned to his squadron. Two weeks later, on April 28, Williams had another close call. He was on a Marine raid of Chinnampo on Korea's west coast. Heavy winds forced the mission closer to the ground than usual and Williams was again an easy target for enemy fire. This time it was anti-aircraft fire. Fortunately, his fuel reserves in the wing did not ignite and he made it back safely.

While in Korea, Ted Williams flew 39 missions. He was awarded an Air Medal and two Gold Stars before receiving a discharge for health reasons in July 1953. He had an inner ear problem that made it impossible for him to remain a pilot. Williams told me during our interview, "I'm no hero. All the guys in our squadron are doing a great job. And same for all the Marines on the MLR. The ground-pounders, they're the real heroes."

Ted Williams returned to the Boston Red Sox lineup after his tour in Korea. His head boss, Tom Yawkey, who was like a father to Williams, wanted him back, as millions of fans did. He was 34 when he returned to baseball on August 6. He played in 37 games in 1953. His final game in baseball was on September 28, 1960 after a 19-year career. His lifetime batting average was .344. He was the last major leaguer to hit .400 in a season. The super-hitter, and war hero, was elected to the Baseball Hall of Fame in 1966. He had the distinction of being inducted into a *second* Hall of Fame, the Marine Corps Sports Hall of Fame, which honors former Marines who have excelled both on and off the athletic playing field.

Ted Williams—"The Kid"—died on July 5, 2002 in Inverness, Florida. He was 83 years old. The Marine Corps and sports fans all over the world will miss one of baseball's best. Ted Williams, the Marine jet pilot and Hall of Famer, is gone, but his legend and most of his records will live on. I was pleased to record the history-making interview on the USS *Haven* in April 1953. I am especially proud to share his story with you.

DOUBLE HONOR

Ted Williams has the distinction of being in two Halls of Fame. First, the Baseball Hall of Fame (1966), then in the Marine Corps' own Hall of Fame, which honors former Marines.

All smiles and stateside is Sgt. Francis (Bud) Grunert, the "Lucky Leatherneck," 1953. The Commandant pulled him off the front line after his close call on October 27, 1952. Captured for three hours, Grunert was saved by two of his buddies. (Photo Courtesy Francis Grunert)

7

THE LUCKY LEATHERNECK

Each morning it was getting colder and harder to leave my sleeping bag. It was October 27, 1952 and just a week before the national election between Dwight D. Eisenhower and Adlai Stevenson. I was at the First Battalion, Seventh Regiment when there was a major attack by the Communist Chinese on the Hook, one of the highest ridges on the Main Line of Resistance. The Hook was one of those positions that changed hands often. It was ours now. One of the Marines on the outpost was Sgt. Francis Grunert, from Trenton, New Jersey. He had arrived in Korea just three weeks before. A 22-year-old squad leader, Grunert was a machine gunner in the First Platoon. He had barely got his .30 caliber machine gun set up when the rifle platoon was overrun by the Communist Chinese. Grunert was grabbed from behind and dragged off by two of the enemy soldiers. A burp gun was pointed at his head as they ran off the ridge and toward the enemy lines. They were about two hundred yards away when two Marine F9 Panther jets started their run to soften up the enemy attack. As the strafing and bombing got closer, the Chinese headed for safety, a small trench, barely big enough for the three of them. To make sure their valuable POW did not get away, the Chinese sat on Grunert. With the enemy on top of him and friendly fire all around him, Grunert had double reason to be worried as hell. Grunert estimated they were in the trench for several hours.

When the jet fighters from the First Marine Air Wing finished their mission, the two Chinese pulled Grunert out of the trench and pointed him toward their lines. They commanded him to place his hands behind his head. Off balance, Grunert was in no position to escape. Suddenly, from out of nowhere, two Marines appeared and startled the enemy. One of the rescuers yanked the young Yank from the Chinese. After a tug-of-war, with Grunert in the middle, he was pulled to freedom. Admitting defeat, the two Chinese, after dropping their weapons, ran like rabbits toward their lines. The two rescuers, with Grunert safely tucked between them, headed for our lines. Francis Grunert had been a prisoner of war for three hours, the longest nightmare in his young life.

Luckily, I was at the First Battalion, Seventh Marines' Regiment when Grunert was brought in. Able Company's commander allowed Grunert to speak with me before his medical exam and the regiment's S-2 Intelligence interrogation. In shock and trembling, he told me he was ready to tell about his ordeal. We sat in the battalion's medical aid tent, where about ten of us were anxious to hear the details. The Battalion Surgeon said to hurry up as he wanted to examine him the minute the taping was over. I suspected that the captain in S-2 was a little pissed off that a radio correspondent got to talk to Grunert before he did.

"Ready, sergeant?" I asked and waved the microphone at him.

I switched on the tape recorder and glanced down to see if the Webcor reel-to-reel recorder was up to speed. Little did I know that this interview would make the media commotion it did, or that the Commandant of the Marine Corps would get involved.

Here is the radio interview as recorded on October 27, 1952. Sgt. Francis Grunert became a Korean War hero, the Lucky Leatherneck, when the story was featured on the *Marine Corps Show* in Hollywood, California, one week later.

IN SHOCK

Still trembling from his ordeal, Sgt. Francis Grunert agreed to an interview. He became a national hero after the broadcast.

HILL: This is Marine Radio Correspondent, Corporal Dick Hill, speaking from a Marine medical aid station close to the front lines of Korea. And with me, probably the luckiest Marine in the Seventh Regiment—in all of Korea—for that matter. Sergeant, would you give your name, please?

GRUNERT: Sergeant Francis Grunert.

HILL: Sergeant Grunert, where's your hometown?

GRUNERT: I'm from Trenton, New Jersey, USA.

HILL: Sergeant, I know you're a little out of breath—and maybe a little shaky—and as I can see, with a few scratches and bruises—but the folks back home—not only in Trenton—Trenton, New Jersey, but all over America would like to hear your story. Something that just happened minutes ago. What did happen to you?

GRUNERT: I was captured by the Communist Chinese. Two of 'em.

HILL: And where did this happen?

GRUNERT: Up on the Hook.

HILL: The Hook? That's one of the ridges on the front lines? On the Main Line of Resistance—the MLR, as you guys call it?

GRUNERT: Yeah! I was just setting up my machine gun when they grabbed me.

HILL: You're a machine gunner? And you're a squad leader, aren't you?

GRUNERT: That's right. Squad leader, First platoon, "Able" Company, First Battalion, Seventh Marine Regiment.

TOUGH DUTY

Grunert was on one of the most dreaded outposts in all Korea – the Hook. If the enemy didn't wound or kill you, they'd capture you.

HILL: You guys in the Seventh Regiment have been busy up on line. That ridge—the Hook—seems like prime property.

GRUNERT: Yeah! It's the highest point around. The gooks want it as much as we do.

HILL: Sergeant...you were setting up your weapon, a machine gun on the Hook. Then what happened?

GRUNERT: The gooks charged our position. They overran us. Must have been a platoon of 'em.

HILL: A platoon? That would be about how many?

GRUNERT: About 50 or so.

HILL: They like to come in big waves, don't they. And according to the two Marines that brought you in, they said the enemy grabbed you from behind?

GRUNERT: Grabbed me from behind and dragged me off. No one else was around.

HILL: Were you ready for the worst? Afraid they'd do more than just capture you?

GRUNERT: Not really. I knew they wanted a prisoner.

HILL: So, they wanted you alive. They get rewards, don't they, if they bring in a prisoner?

GRUNERT: That's right. They do. Especially when you're a Marine. We've been told this.

HILL: What happened next? After they pulled you off the front lines?

GRUNERT: They put a burp gun to my head. And made me run with them off the line. And toward their lines. Then all hell broke loose.

HILL: All hell broke loose? What happened?

GRUNERT: That's when our fighter jets came in strafing and bombing.

HILL: Where were you? Past your lines? Out in no man's land? Between the MLR and the Chinese lines?

GRUNERT: Something like that. I was a little groggy. We were way past our lines by now. We were catching a lot of flak all around us. The Chinese guys were as scared as I was. They wanted to get out of there. They found a trench. Really more of a ditch than anything else. We dived in it for protection. Then the damn guys sat on me.

HILL: Sat on you? You're kidding!

GRUNERT: They sat on me so I wouldn't get away.

HILL: Maybe that was good. It gave you some protection from all the "friendly fire" from the Marine air strike. How close did the bombing get to you? Was it close?

GRUNERT: Close enough. Maybe a hundred yards or so.

HILL: Ohhhhhh! That's close! What was worse? The enemy on top of you? Or the jets with that air strike all around you? And with you right in the middle of it all?

GRUNERT: This may sound funny. I was more afraid of our own jet fighters than the two Chinese sitting on me. I was hoping for our pilots to quit their mission.

HILL: How long were you in the trench...or ditch as you called it?

GRUNERT: It seemed like hours—until the air strike finally lifted.

HILL: Then you left the ditch, or trench. Left your safety cover...then what?

Many of my buddies revisited Korea after the war. Seoul was a mass of skycrapers rather than of rubble. It was an emotional experience. Especially after touring the remnants of trenches and bunkers where they fought.

105

Sgt. Francis Grunert, squad leader, with his .30 caliber machine gun in the 7th Regiment's reserve area, 1952. (Photo Courtesy Francis Grunert)

GRUNERT: Then we got up and they made me keep my hands behind my head. They had a burp gun at my back. It was hard to run. Hard to keep my balance. I kept falling. They didn't like that.

HILL: And you were headed toward the Chinese lines then?

GRUNERT: Right! I was. And it wasn't a good feeling.

HILL: I'm sure it wasn't. Then I understand the unexpected happened. Your luck suddenly turned around. What happened?

GRUNERT: Thank God it did. Two of my buddies had followed us. One grabbed me away from the gooks. Then the gook grabbed back. My combat vest nearly fell apart.

HILL: Sounds like a tug-of-war. With you in the middle.

GRUNERT: There was lots of shoving—and pulling—fighting. I was finally pulled away from those guys. Then they started running.

HILL: Running? Running toward their lines?

GRUNERT: Right. Toward their lines. One even dropped his weapon. Then they started running toward their lines.

HILL: And what did you guys do?

GRUNERT: That's what we did, too. Started running back to our line.

HILL: Kind of a "they went their way and you went your way" situation. Could the Chinese soldiers that had you—could they speak any English?

GRUNERT: No. Only their gobbly-gook—Chinese. But they did know one word.

HILL: One word? What was that?

GRUNERT: Marine. They knew I was a Marine.

HILL: We can make light of it now. But they thought they had a gold mine. A real, U.S. Marine prisoner. Thank God it never materialized. How do you feel now, sergeant, back of the lines. Back at battalion. Among friends, I might add.

GRUNERT: A great feeling. Nothing better.

HILL: And true to tradition—a couple of Marine buddies came off the lines to rescue you.

GRUNERT: They sure did. Else we wouldn't be talking now.

HILL: Sergeant Grunert? You were captive for about how long. (Pause.). About how long were you in enemy hands?

GRUNERT: Hard to say. Couple of hours, anyway.

HILL: Sergeant Francis Grunert, from Trenton, New Jersey, you sure earned your combat pay today. And thankfully, we can all celebrate the happy ending to your ordeal, today. Thank you for taking time to share your story. A lot of people will be thinking about you and your fellow Marines—and about the tough job you're doing here in Korea. Best of luck in the future. This is Marine Radio Correspondent Corporal Dick Hill saying it's been my honor to be speaking with a very "Lucky Leatherneck," Sergeant Francis Grunert, with the Seventh Marine Regiment. Broadcasting from Korea, we now return you to the *Marine Corps Show* in Hollywood, California.

REUNION

Some 50 years after recording Francis Grunert, I talked to him by phone. "Hey, I remember you," he said. "You made me a hero with your radio broadcast." Correction. Grunert made himself a hero.

Within hours of the national broadcast of Grunert's story, the New York media raced to his parents' home in Trenton, New Jersey. Reporters from the *New York Times, New York Herald Tribune* and *Philadelphia Inquirer* all wrote stories about the area hero who was a POW for three hours. The *Journal* sent their star columnist, Dorothy Kilgallen, who was also famous for her television appearances on *What's My Line?* Much to the surprise of Miss Kilgallen, Grunert's mother had not heard the broadcast, nor did she know about her son's short-term capture. She fainted when told so. Grunert's family corresponded with me soon after. I brought them up to speed and sent them a copy of the taped interview. The family was gracious and grateful.

The Commandant of the Marine Corps, Lemuel C. Shepherd, Jr., wanted Korea's newest hero pulled off the front lines, at least until he recuperated from the shock of his close call. Grunert was lucky—fantastically lucky—on the day of his capture. Eighteen of his comrades in the First Platoon, Able Company, First Battalion, Seventh Regiment were casualties in the same battle with the Chinese that day. Six were killed in action and twelve were wounded. The enemy suffered with 40 casualties.

I keep in touch with Grunert. He retired as a GySgt. after a 20-year career with the Marines. Today he lives in Lake Panasoffkee, Florida, where he enjoys fishing. He is a valued member of the "A/1/7 Marine Corps Association – Korea 1950–53." The nearly 200 members look forward to their quarterly newsletters and special reunion each year. The wives will tell you there is more battle talk during their get-togethers than with any other Marine Corps association.

Stable Able was one hell of an outfit. To learn more about Able Company and its A/1/7 association, please visit: *http://home.planetcomm.net/StableAble17/*.

Dorothy Kilgallen, the journalist who interviewed Grunert's mother, died suddenly in 1965. She had been investigating the assassination of President John F. Kennedy. She had interviewed Jack Ruby during a recess of his trial for the shooting death of Lee Harvey Oswald. Her newspaper column was critical of the Warren Commission that investigated President Kennedy's assassination. She wrote: "This story isn't going to die as long as there's a real reporter alive." Some people believe that she was murdered by members of the alleged JFK conspiracy.

During Kilgallen's famous career as a journalist, she wrote countless stories that caught the public's attention, including the memorable piece that helped tag Sgt. Francis Grunert "the Lucky Leatherneck." The name has stuck to this day.

Nearly 50 years after his narrow escpe in Korea, Francis Grunert, in Lake Panasoffkee, Florida, 2001. (Photo Courtesy Francis Grunert)

The author in Seoul, January 1953. Sadly, the warm thermo (Mickey Mouse) boots weren't available for the Chosin Reservoir Marines in December 1950. (Author's Collection)

8

KOREA'S SECOND ENEMY

Having been raised in Minnesota, I had a slight advantage when it came to the cold winters in Korea. I did not enjoy temperatures 20 to 30 degrees below zero, but I had experienced them before. Lots of the men from below the Mason-Dixon line could not get used to them. When I first arrived at the First Marine Division headquarters, a gunny sergeant from the Bible Belt told me, "If the snipers, mortars, or artillery did not get you, the winter will."

The worst of winters was in 1950 during the Chosin Reservoir battle. There were 12,000 casualties, including thousands of severe frostbite cases from the minus-30-degree temperatures. Sadly, the Marines did not have all the proper cold-weather gear they needed. Thermo boots, or Mickey Mouse boots, as the guys in my tent called them, did not reach the troops until 1951. They helped a lot. Some of the best advice the platoon leaders ever gave was, "Keep your feet dry, change your socks, and don't get frostbite." Frozen toes and feet were not a pretty sight.

William B. Hopkins tells about the killing cold in his book *One Bugle No Drums*. A Marine Captain during the war, Hopkins commanded the H&S (Headquarters & Service) Company, First Battalion, First Marine Division. He describes "the second enemy" he and his men faced:

> The Seventh Regiment's experience had revealed a second enemy even more devastating than the Chinese Communists, however—the cold. Daily morning reports listed Marines suffering frostbite, in some cases very severely. Frostbite is an injury to the skin or underlying tissue where actual freezing occurs; mild frostbite produces only swelling and reddening of the skin, but severe cases affect deep tissues, including bone, which may culminate in loss of the frozen part.

Another Korean War Marine, James Brady, has written several books on his experiences. In *The Coldest War*, he tells how the winter affected him and the men in his platoon:

HOT CHOW

Whenever possible, Marines got a hot meal up on line. It was something to look forward to during those cold, bitter days. You'd get steak, fried potatoes, pancakes, eggs, and real hot coffee.

> There were men with rheumatism from the wet months and sleeping on the ground. And men who coughed and spit up blood. And men who'd been frostbitten early and had to keep those parts covered the best way they could because the tissue was damaged and would be susceptible afterward. That happened to my ears, both of them, the lobes. None of these things qualified you for medical evacuation. You tried to heal them yourself, or asked the corpsman, and you stayed up on line.

If the winter was brutal for tested Marines, what was it like for Marguerite Higgins, the first woman war correspondent to cover the Korean War and a top reporter with the *New York Herald Tribune*? Here's what she said about those cold, Manchurian winds by the Chosin Reservoir in December 1950: "The frost and wind howling through the narrow pass were almost as deadly as the enemy."

Miss Higgins knew what she was talking about. She was with the Marines during their "advance to the rear," the road back from the Chosin Reservoir, over which the Marines had to plunge fifteen miles through ice and snow and enemy line. She saw first-hand what the bone chilling weather did to young Marines and others.

Blame the weather on the monsoons. These seasonal winds affect the weather throughout the year. A monsoon blows in from the south and southeast during the summer. These I call the friendly monsoons. They brought in the hot, humid 80-degree days that I experienced my first summer in Korea. But, God, it was those wicked winds in the winter that were killers. They came out of Siberia and Manchuria from the north. Snow and sleet came in off the Sea of Japan from the east. Often we'd see up to two or three feet or more of snow from one storm.

New thermo boots in 1951 were a godsend for Korean winters.

To find out how the fighting men in the Seventh Marine Regiment withstood winter in Korea, I took my tape recorder to them. The participants in the interview are Cpl. George Whitledge, St. Louis, Missouri; Pfc. Everett Locke, Camas, Washington; Cpl. Neimand L. Durham, Grandview, Washington; Cpl. William Post, North Redding, Massachusetts; and Pfc. Emmet Potts from Zanesville, Ohio. Below is a transcript of a broadcast from early December 1952 that aired on the *Marine Corps Show* from Hollywood, California. Millions of people heard this story and became more aware of the "second enemy" that the military faced in Korea:

HILL: Speaking from the fighting front of the First Marine Division in Korea, this is Marine Radio Correspondent, Dick Hill. With the arrival of winter, Marines discovered that cold weather can prove to be more deadly than the enemy. This marks the third winter that Marines have experienced in the frozen fields of Korea. Every step has been taken to see that the men have the best type of clothing for the freezing temperatures. To give our listeners some idea of how the Marines survive the winter in Korea, we took our tape recorder up and down the front lines. We first stopped and asked a young corporal what he thought of the cold-weather clothing. Without hesitating, he answered:

WHITLEDGE: It's great. I don't know what we'd do without our winter clothing.

HILL: Corporal, would you give your name and hometown, please?

WHITLEDGE: Sure. I'm George Whitledge from St. Louis, Missouri.

HILL: George, what about the cold-weather gear? What exactly do you have?

WHITLEDGE: We have thermal boots, parkas, long underwear, wool trousers, wool sweaters, wool caps, gloves and mufflers.

HILL: Sounds like a wardrobe for an Eskimo.

WHITLEDGE: It is. Sure keeps us warm.

HILL: George, what about these thermal boots you mentioned?

WHITLEDGE: Oh, our Mickey Mouse boots. They're wonderful. I don't know what we'd do without them. They keep your feet warm even on the coldest days.

HILL: I might add that they do look like Mickey Mouse's boots. What do you wear inside them?

WHITLEDGE: Well, I've only worn one pair of socks, myself. Some guys wear two pair.

HILL: Thanks to the clothing that Cpl. George Whitledge, from St. Louis, Missouri, talked about, Marines will eliminate any number of cold weather casualties. And with this same type of winter gear, Marines continue patrols into enemy territory, despite the freezing temperatures. Regardless of the season, the purpose of the patrol remains the same. Search out the enemy and destroy him. With me now is Private First Class Everett Locke. How do you like this patrol work in winter?

LOCKE: Well, it is pretty cold now, but we all feel it is a job we've got to do.

HILL: How long are your scouting patrols?

LOCKE: We usually scout around four hours.

HILL: And I bet that last summer it was hard to visualize that it would ever be so cold this winter.

LOCKE: Sure was. But we did not think too much about it then.

HILL: Well, Pfc. Locke, how do you stay warm when you're past the lines?

LOCKE: We wear a lot of cold-weather gear. And we keep moving most of the time. That helps.

HILL: And what about camouflage?

LOCKE: We wear a white uniform that blends in with snow. It's pretty good concealment.

HILL: Pfc. Everett Locke, I think I forgot to ask where you're from.

LOCKE: From Washington State. Camas, Washington.

HILL: Well, I certainly wish you luck for the rest of your tour here in Korea. And let's hope it won't be too long before you're back in Camas, Washington, going strolling with that special gal of yours. (Pause.) A motor transport unit in Korea requires a couple of items in the winter. Plenty of antifreeze for its many trucks and jeeps. And an ample supply of aspirin for all the headaches that come with the freezing weather in Korea. Corporal Neimand L. Durham from Grandview, Washington, knows what I'm talking about.

Dressed for the Korean winter, the author interviews a 7th Regiment Marine in 1952. (Marine Corps Photo)

How long have you been driving here in Korea, corporal?

DURHAM: I've been driving jeeps and trucks for nine months. The roads in the summertime are rough enough. But the winter is a big headache as far as driving is concerned.

HILL: Do you have heaters in the vehicles?

DURHAM: Yes. In most of them. But the coldest weather can keep them from functioning one-hundred percent. It's usually the thermostats that give the motor pool mechanics the most trouble. They have to keep tinkering with them most of the winter.

HILL: What about the roads, corporal? The roads in the winter, that is.

DURHAM: (Laughs.) Ever try to drive over a washboard? The roads are double rough in the winter. The sun doesn't get to some parts of the roads—and they don't thaw out for quite a while.

HILL: What's this about you going home pretty soon?

DURHAM: In the spring I'll be rotating. By then it'll be a heck of a lot easier driving for the rest of my buddies.

HILL: Good luck to you, Corporal Neimand Durham. And it won't be long before you'll be driving down a nice, smooth highway back home in Grandview, Washington. (Pause.) When the first cold spell hit Korea a couple of months back, Marines were hurrying to line their bunkers and tents to give it that extra-needed insulation for winter. Now, a few months later, it is beginning to pay off. Any frontline Marine will vouch for the value of a warm bunker after coming in from guard duty, or fighting from a freezing foxhole.

These are the Marines who can tell you how a bunker will not only keep them warm, but protect them from enemy fire. These are the men who are fighting for you in Korea:

POST: I'm William Post from North Redding, Massachusetts. I'm a radioman. And I'll sure be glad when this winter's over.

HILL: Corporal William Post, tell us about sleeping conditions in winter.

POST: It's not too bad. We have pretty good sleeping bags that we use in the bunkers.

HILL: And what about recreation?

POST: Well, there isn't too much time for that. But we do get a card game in once in a while.

HILL: Marines like their cards, don't they?

POST: Sure do. Especially in winter. There isn't a bunker or a tent without a deck or two.

HILL: How long have you been in Korea?

POST: Just about nine months.

HILL: Nine months. That means in a few months you'll be going home. Look for him, you folks in the North Redding, Massachusetts area—look for Corporal William Post. He's coming your way. Now from a Marine named Post we go to a Marine called Potts...

POTTS: My name is Pfc. Emmett Potts from Zanesville, Ohio.

HILL: Pfc. Emmett Potts, what outfit are you with?

POTTS: I'm with 4.2 Mortars, Seventh Regiment.

HILL: And I might put a plug in for you fellows with the Seventh Regiment. You sure stay busy don't you? And how's winter treating you?

David Douglas Duncan, photojournalist with Life *magazine, experienced the bitter-cold Chosin march to safety with the Marines and other UN forces in December 1950. (Photography Collection, Harry Ransom-Humanities Research Center, The University of Texas at Austin)*

117

YUKON GOLD

Marines guarded them with their lives—the oil burning Yukon Stoves that took the chill out of winter.

POTTS: Yeah. Very busy. But that's what we're over here for. And regarding winter, it is just something we have to put up with.

HILL: Emmett, would you give the folks back home a description of your bunker that we're recording from at the present time?

POTTS: Sure. It's a three-man bunker on the MLR. MLR, that's the Main Line of Resistance. And we have a Yukon stove in one corner. It keeps us plenty warm.

HILL: Oil burning, aren't they? Does every bunker have a Yukon stove, like you do?

POTTS: Well, if the guys that live in it are lucky enough to get one. They're hard to find.

HILL: Ohhhh. A little Marine requisition, huh? What do you have your bunker lined with?

POTTS: That was one of the guys' ideas. We've lined it with blankets to keep the cold out.

HILL: Good idea. Seems to be working. Nice 'n' cozy in here. How's the chow in winter, Emmett?

POTTS: Well, occasionally we get a hot meal brought up to the front lines. Pretty good. Other times we've got our old standby—C-Rations.

HILL: Thank you, Pfc. Emmett Potts, for allowing us in your frontline bunker. We wish you the best of luck during your remaining time in Korea—before returning to Zanesville, Ohio.

And we hope that some day soon all the troops will be back to their hometowns. The winter in Korea is cold. But along with all the cold-weather gear to help fight Korea's second enemy—the bone chilling winter—the men have the flame of freedom burning in their bunkers and trenches. The same flame that has burned throughout the years in the hearts of all people who wish to halt enemy aggression. And achieve freedom. This is Marine Radio Correspondent Dick Hill speaking from the Seventh Regiment in Korea. We return you now to the *Marine Corps Show* in Hollywood, California.

———————————

After this story was broadcast, my tent buddies swear they saw a surge of scarves, mittens, and earmuffs, arriving in the mail. Lots of Campbell's soup and Hershey's cocoa arrived, too. MSgt. H.B. Wells, a combat photographer, facetiously said, "Seeing all the cold-weather clothing and food come in, Hill, your radio listeners seem to be anxious to fulfill all our needs. Now maybe you could put a plug in for more toilet paper—something we *really* need."

David Douglas Duncan holding a Rolleiflex camera with Heiland flashgun. El Toro Marine Corps Air Station, 1943. (Photography Collection, Harry Ranson-Humanities Research Center, The University of Texas at Austin)

9

PHOTOJOURNALISTS

My dad and I were having a slice of apple pie à la mode when I saw the picture. We were at the Chef Cafe, a popular neighborhood coffee shop, on Franklin and Chicago Avenue in Minneapolis. It was 1945 and I was 14, in Phillips Junior High School. My dad was scanning the *Tribune* when I saw it on the front page: The raising of the American flag on Mount Suribachi during the battle of Iwo Jima.

"Wow!" I told my dad. "I'd like to take pictures like that."

"So would everyone," my father responded. "But that is a once-in-a-lifetime photo."

Apparently he had admired it too while reading the front page. He flipped the paper around to look at it one more time. Then commented: "It is a nice climax for all that damn fighting the Marines had to go through on Iwo Jima."

The Marines are the source for many memorable photos in war. The flag-raising photo atop Mount Suribachi, for example, has become the most reproduced image in the world. It was taken by a civilian war correspondent, Joe Rosenthal, an Associated Press photographer. He was turned down by the Army because of bad eyesight, so he joined AP instead. He won a Pulitzer Prize in 1945 for the picture. It was described by the Pulitzer Prize committee as "one of the great moments—a frozen flash of history—caught by a camera."

I found out from one of our photographers in Korea that Rosenthal used the traditional Speed Graphic camera. Press people and the military loved that big, old, heavy, but dependable, camera. Eastman Kodak had developed it years before. Photography buffs, take note: I learned that Rosenthal's camera's exposure was

After my tour in Korea, I had a bumper sticker on my 1953 Ford Crestliner that read: "Honk if you like MARINES." I had to scrape it off. It created too many "hits."

1/400th of a second, with the f-stop between 8 and 16. As MSgt. Wells, an excellent Combat Photographer himself, told me, it was the perfect lens setting for the award-winning photo we still admire today.

The picture was taken on February 23, 1945. It showed five Marines and a Navy Corpsman raising the American flag. It was a thing of beauty. The makeshift flag pole looked heavy. But together, as a group, they could handle it. My boot camp DI, Sgt. H.J. Fuller, who had served on Iwo Jima, called it "the epitome of teamwork." Three of the participants were killed in battle. The survivors received orders to come back to the states for a promotional war bond tour around the country. The public welcomed the heroes enthusiastically as they helped raise millions of dollars for the government.

That history-making photo sparked my interest in photojournalism. I guess that is why I instinctively struck up close friendships with our PIO photo guys in Korea. My impression was that photojournalists are a special breed. They are gutsy, independent and skilled at war photography. The ones I knew had no qualms about risking their lives to get frontline pictures. While getting that "perfect shot," they were oblivious to the surrounding danger to their own lives. During my tour in 1952–1953, the photographers assigned to PIO Headquarters were MSgt. Jim Galloway, TSgt. Robert Kiser and MSgt. Harold (H.B.) Wells. And there were many more scattered throughout the division and at the First Marine Air Wing. H.B. Wells invited me to try his 4 X 5 Speed Graphic for a few shots. It became the standard for press people. Heavy, compared to my little Kodak, it took great pictures. Fortunately for history buffs, the photos from the Korean War still "live" today.

War photographers have learned that to capture the most powerful images, you have to throw yourself in the middle of battle. Robert Capa, one of the premiere war photographers, may have said it best: "If your pictures aren't good enough," he said, "you're not close enough." David Douglas Duncan, a *Life* magazine photographer like Capa, had the same philosophy. Duncan produced some of the best Korean War images, as showcased in his book, *This Is War!*, first published in 1951.

In the early days of Korea, the Marines needed more firepower than photos. So Sgt. Frank C. Kerr, following the Marine creed, "Always a rifleman first," favored his M1 rifle over his camera. From Massachusetts, Kerr served as both rifleman and Combat Correspondent in three key battles in Korea: The Pusan Perimeter, Inchon landing and Chosin Reservoir. His photos from the Chosin retreat are a permanent reminder of the price the United Nations forces paid for General Douglas MacArthur's mistake of underestimating the Communist Chinese. Despite evidence the Marines and the U.S. Eighth Army forwarded to his command in Tokyo about captured Chinese soldiers saying, "There's more to come," MacArthur advised President Truman and the Joint Chiefs of Staff that the Chinese would never enter the war. Further, he said that the U.S. troops would be home for Christmas.

MOVE TO THE FRONT

"If your picures aren't good enough, you aren't close enough."

–Robert Capa, Photojournalist

U.S. Marines raise the American flag atop Mount Suribachi, Iwo Jima, February 23, 1945. This photo is the most reproduced image in the world and won a Pulitzer Prize for the AP photographer, Joe Rosenthal. (AP Photo/Joe Rosenthal)

At the Chosin Reservoir, Kerr and roughly 15,000 Allied ground forces—mostly elements of the First Marine Division, along with a regimental combat team of the Army's Seventh Infantry Division, a small unit of the British Royal Marine Commandos and South Korean troops—ran into the "Red Tide" of Chinese. Masses of Chinese soldiers crossed the Manchurian border and entered the war on November 27, 1950. On that Thanksgiving Day, 200,000 Chinese took the Allies by surprise. They routed the U.S. Eighth Army and surrounded 10,000 Marines of the First Marine Division at the Chosin Reservoir.

Young Sgt. Kerr and his fellow Marines were led by the storied Brig. Gen. Lewis B. "Chesty" Puller. Their fighting withdrawal to safety from November 27 to December 9 is considered by many to be one of the more harrowing campaigns in U.S. military history. They fought their way out—Kerr firing both his M1 and shooting pictures—on a mountainous road in sub-arctic conditions. (For the full story, see the chapter entitled *The Red Tide*.)

Those veteran Marines have called themselves the "Chosin Few" ever since and formed an association by that name. It is only fitting that one of the co-founders is former Marine photojournalist, Frank Kerr. Navy Corpsman John F. Hessman, is the other.

Can those Speed Graphics be eligible for a Purple Heart? That is what some of the photojournalists were facetiously wondering when a buddy of theirs had a camera shot up. I had not met Sgt. Angelo R. Caramico, but I sure heard about his close call. On January 9,

DOUBLE DUTY

Frank Kerr, combat photographer, spent more time using his M1 rifle than his Speed Graphic camera. He was part of the unit coming out of the Chosin Reservoir. Many of his pictures are in the National Archives.

The famous Kodak 4 X 5 Speed Graphic camera that combat photographers carried all over Korea. (Author's Collection)

1952, a few months before I arrived in Korea, he was assigned to get photos of an "empty" enemy bunker up on the front lines. To his surprise, the fortress was still occupied by enemy soldiers. Caramico knew when he was not invited to get out of there—fast! And he did. But during the scramble, a sniper fired at him, and missed, but hit the bed of his Speed Graphic. And he has a photo to prove it.

"Damn," Caramico thought to himself. "They may have messed up my camera. I wished they had winged me, instead. I can be patched up easier that that damn temperamental camera of mine."

Almost from the very first day of the Korean conflict, another photographer whom I had heard about, David Douglas Duncan, was busy still-shooting the war. I remembered his eye-catching picture spreads in *Life* magazine from years before. A former Marine CC in World War II, D.D.D., as he was known by his monogram, is considered one of the best photojournalists in the world. On June 25, 1950, when the North Koreans crashed over the 38th Parallel to trigger the war, Duncan was in Tokyo, just a two-hour plane ride away from some of the great photos we were soon to see in *Life* magazine and his book. Learning of the pending international war, David Douglas Duncan, this time as a civilian, was packed and ready to shoot his second war—Korea. Transportation was scarce. But the press have a way of getting to their destination. He hitched a ride on the next C-47 out of Japan.

Something conspicuously missing when D.D.D. landed at Kimpo field, near Seoul, were Speed Graphic and Rolleiflex cameras. Instead, slung around his neck were two 35mm German-made Leica cameras fitted with Japanese-made Nikkor lenses. Prior to the Korean War, he had experimented with the Nikkor lenses, made in occupied Japan. Impressed with the superior results from these high-tech cameras and lenses, D.D.D. decided his new discovery was the way to go.

For more on this daring move away from Eastman Kodak's proven Speed Graphic camera, here is an except that appeared in the book that Marines treasure in their library, *Last to Know, First to Go,* by Garry Cameron. Both Cameron and David Douglas Duncan were Combat Correspondents:

35MM REVOLUTION

David Douglas Duncan, former Marine and Life *photographer, led the industry with his 35mm camera. It produced sharper images than the Speed Graphic and Rolleiflex cameras.*

When the drive to the Chosin Reservoir kicked off, the PIO section evolved a system whereby a 35mm movie cameraman and two 16mm movie men, shooting color film, were assigned to each regiment. The bulky and relatively sensitive Speed Graphic cameras they were issued inhibited still-photo men in moving situations. It took the innovation and talent of a WWII CC, David Douglas Duncan, who was covering Korean combat in civilian status, to show which equipment was the most suitable. With his 35mm still camera—Leica bodies and Nikkor lenses—he covered the First Marine Division. The resulting book, *This Is War!,* was immediately a success and is now a classic.

Not only were the small and rugged cameras used to their best advantage, but chemicals and film had improved tremendously over the years. The lab technicians at *Life* magazine, who processed many of

Duncan's films, were so good they could take film that was not the best and turn out useable and vivid photos. In some cases when D.D.D. had indicated the film was fogged, out of focus, etc., they would develop it anyway and, in several instances, screening a print, turned the result into an art form.

There is no doubt that Duncan was the leader in photojournalism techniques that were required to effectively cover combat and the men at war. However, it took a number of years and another war before hardened civilian journalists would be seen with 35mm cameras slung around their necks.

I have in my humble library a copy of David Douglas Duncan's book, *This Is War! A Photo-Narrative of the Korean War*. And like Garry Cameron says in *Last to Know, First to Go*, it is a classic. It is dog-eared from my constant admiration. How he achieved some of the photos I am sure has been discussed in photojournalism classes. Never in the history of books has an artist—be they writer, painter or photographer—brought the actuality of war closer to the reader than David Douglas Duncan. His photo-narrative on the Korean War—*This Is War!*—was a breakthrough in publishing. I'm proud to include many of Duncan's photos in *Battle Talk!*

Just as D.D.D. pioneered the use of the smaller, lighter, high-tech 35mm still cameras over those bulky Speed Graphics, the evolution continues. Look what digital cameras are doing to 35mm cameras and the film industry. We are a lucky generation. We are in the midst of the greatest revolution in photography and

image-making since Kodak first invented its popular
Brownie camera over a hundred years ago.

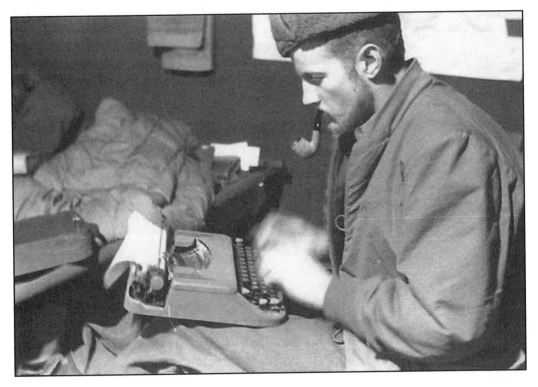

Marine Combat Correspondent Frank Praytor finishes a story on his trusty Smith Co-rona.

With the aid of a South Korean interpreter, a Marine interrogates two Chinese prisoners near the Chosin Reservoir in 1950. Later in the war, Psychological Warfare broadcasts helped snag enemy soldiers. (Photo Courtesy Doubleday and Company)

10

PSYWAR

History was being made during one of my radio interviews in January 1953. It was the first time the Marine Psychological Warfare Operation (PSYOP or PSYWAR) shared its mission in Korea. I received premission to broadcast one of its operations. I will never forget it.

It was cold, dark, and a little tense with all the incoming mortar fire that we were attracting from the enemy Chinese. (They were targeting the loudspeakers broadcasting our messages in Chinese.) The interview with Sgt. Ward Gilliam, G-2, Intelligence Section, took place in a captured, unheated Chinese bunker. It is important to understand something about psychological warfare before getting to the transcript of the radio interview that took place on the front lines of Korea.

A psychological warfare campaign is a war of the mind. In boot camp I learned that the primary weapons are sight and sound. PSYWAR can be disseminated by face-to-face communication, audio visual means (television), audio media (radio or loudspeaker), and visual media (leaflets, newspapers, books, or posters.) The weapon is not the means or medium, but the message it carries and how that message affects the recipient. Radio broadcasts became a major means of passing propaganda to the enemy. Japan used the notorious "Tokyo Rose" in World War II to broadcast discouragement to our allied forces. Ditto for "Hanoi Hannah" in Vietnam. In the Gulf War, "Baghdad Betty" tried to unravel our troops.

Tactical PSYWAR is addressed to a specific enemy combat group to induce them to perform a specific action that will affect the current or short-range combat situation, such as reducing morale and combatting efficiency within the enemy's ranks. Psychological warfare is not a new military tactic by any means. There are numerous examples throughout history. One of the earliest was attributed to Alexander the Great of Macedonia. Alexander had conquered most of the known world during his reign. With each region he conquered, he left behind soldiers to keep control of the newly secured area. Eventually, there came a point when Alexander realized he had stretched his army too thin and was in danger of losing to a large opposing force. His only option was to retreat and regroup forces with the armies he left behind. Yet to do so would certainly incite the opposing force to pursue him and very possibly capture or defeat his now-smaller army.

Alexander knew that if he could intimidate the opposing force, it would be scared to follow his army. He instructed his armorers to make several oversized armor breastplates and helmets that would fit "giants," men seven to eight feet tall. As Alexander and his forces withdrew during the night, they left behind the oversized armor. It was found by the opposing force who then believed that they had come close to engaging in a battle with giants, a battle that they surely would have lost. The oversized armor, coupled with the stories they had heard from travelers of the savagery of Alexander's army, caused enough doubt and fear that they elected not to pursue Alexander.

Having learned the effectiveness of radio broadcasts and leaflets during World War II, the U.S. Army Far East Command's small Special Projects Branch of the Headquarters G-2 (Intelligence) Division began radio broadcasts and leaflet drops over the Republic of South Korea immediately after North Korea's invasion across the 38th parallel in June 1950. Later, during the fall of

that year, the First Loudspeaker and Leaflet Company arrived in South Korea. This unit would serve as the Eighth Army's tactical-psychological warfare unit until the end of the war on July 27, 1953.

Leaving most of the PSYWAR to the U.S. Army, the Marines did initiate Operation Backlash in December 1952. The Marines wanted to weaken the Communist Chinese soldiers' morale in the Marines' sector by getting enemy soldiers to think about their home, family, and women.

Sgt. Ward Gilliam, from Richmond, Virginia, was in charge of the G-2 (Intelligence) project. Here is the transcript from the radio interview taped in December 1952 that was broadcast on the *Marine Corps Show* from Hollywood, California:

A frontline three-man sleeping bunker, similar to the enemy bunker where the author recorded the Marine Corps' first PSY-WAR broadcast. (Author's Collection)

THOSE DAMN BUGLES

"The enemy used PSY-WAR, too. Starting with their jarring Chinese bugles."

—Sgt. Ward Gilliam, G-2, Intelligence

SOUND: Speakers playing chinese music.

HILL: (Over music.) From the snow-covered mountaintops somewhere on the western front in Korea, this is Marine Radio Correspondent Dick Hill. At the moment, we have our portable tape recorder set up on one of the frontline positions to bring you an on-the-spot account of a Marine Psychological Warfare team in action. And right now, Sergeant Ward Gilliam of Richmond, Virginia, who is in charge of this project, is getting one of his nightly Chinese language broadcasts to the opposing communists' forces in this sector. Sergeant Gilliam, would you give us some idea of the approximate distance from here to the enemy positions across the way?

GILLIAM: Yes, Dick. In Marine Corps terms, it is about 1500 meters, which in civilian language would be about 1700 yards.

HILL: Sergeant, I notice right now that the speaker has been turned on. And there's a Korean interpreter addressing the Chinese troops. But first, I understand that your time is up as far as rotation is concerned in Korea. But you stayed over. That you found this assignment rather interesting. And you realize that it is doing something for the morale for our troops, and doing something to help win the war. How much longer are you going to prolong your stay here in Korea?

GILLIAM: Yes, I plan to stay an extra six months. Since this work is most interesting—and we hope productive. It is one of the finer jobs I've had in the Marine Corps.

HILL: I might mention to the folks back home that we're located in a Chinese bunker. Is that right?

SOUND: Enemy sniper fire.

GILLIAM: Yes. This is an enemy bunker. It was used by the Chinese Army sometime back. It has been abandoned by our troops, because they will not live in bunkers that the enemy has used—unless absolutely necessary.

HILL: Well, sergeant, I wonder if you could give the people back home some idea of the purpose of psychological warfare.

GILLIAM: Our main purpose, of course, is to catch prisoners. But we have other reasons, too. One is to decrease the efficiency of enemy units. Another is to knock out guerrilla activities and many others. Some are too detailed to go into.

HILL: Do you have a particular title for this operation that you're working on right now?

GILLIAM: Yes. This is a 30-day operation. It's titled "Backlash."

HILL: Could you explain something about "Operation: Backlash?"

GILLIAM: Well, for the first six days we have played nothing to the Chinese but music. Old Chinese folk songs. For the next fourteen days we're going into the propaganda end of it. We are talking and telling these people little ways in which they can goof off and slow down the efficiency of the enemy unit across the way.

HILL: Sergeant, would you relay to the folks back home our position? And the location of the speaker that is playing the Chinese interpretations?

SOUND: Enemy sniper fire.

GILLIAM: Sure. Our loudspeaker is about 50 yards in front of the lines. Our tape recorder, which we are

Sgt. Ward Gilliam turned down his rotation rights to go home and stayed in Korea another six months to continue his PSYWAR projects. He felt his work could help end the war sooner.

now recording on, is about 50 yards behind it. And our amplifier, generator and tape recorder, which is carrying our message to the Chinese, is about 200 yards back of us.

HILL: In other words, Sergeant Gilliam, right now we're on the front lines and the enemy—the Communist Chinese—are hopefully listening to your psychological warfare message. What reaction do you get from the Chinese when you play these tapes over the loudspeaker?

GILLIAM: Once in a while we get a considerable incoming fire. Especially when the propaganda end of it is working.

HILL: And by incoming, you mean what? Mortar or sniper fire?

GILLIAM: Yes. Both. Mortar, sometimes artillery. And small arms, or sniper fire. We get 'em all.

HILL: Sergeant, what exactly is on these tapes that you broadcast over the loud speaker?

GILLIAM: We have many types of tapes we use. Tonight, for instance, we are using news items. Current news happening around the world. Mostly, of course, happenings in China and areas which are familiar to these people. Then we have that music. Chinese folk songs.

HILL: Are they listening?

GILLIAM: Yes. We know that. These people across the way here are pretty active in counteracting our broadcast. They have on occasion broadcast back to us.

HILL: Really?

GILLIAM: Yes! The last few days we've had a broadcast, they did the same. Some of those were around

Christmastime. They played Christmas carols and also made many statements, which amused our boys greatly.

HILL: So, they played music to you; now you're playing some back to them. Kind of tit for tat.

GILLIAM: Right. That's why we moved into this area. Seems to be a good one for getting our message across.

HILL: Sergeant, what protection do you take? For your protection—and the protection of your equipment?

GILLIAM: Well, for myself, I've got my flak jacket and helmet, like all the men up on line wear. And we work from this bunker, which is pretty secure. But our speaker is entirely unprotected. It is right out in the open. And sometimes it does get shot up considerably.

HILL: So, every once in while you have to leave the bunker. And get out the mending tape, as far as the speaker wire is concerned. And you do a little patching on it? That has to be a little risky.

GILLIAM: You got it. But we do it fast. Tonight, for instance, we did have our lines cut. From some fragments of mortar fire. Just before we started this recording with you.

HILL: How does the cold weather affect your broadcasting?

GILLIAM: The Korean winter sure doesn't help. You know about that. It is the amplifier that's most delicate. The tubes sometimes crack in the freezing temperatures. And it takes a while to warm up our recorder, also.

HILL: How long has this project been going on?

137

GILLIAM: Well, this is something new for the Marine Corps. We've only been in operation about a month. We're trying to start up a Psychological Warfare Department in the Marines.

HILL: Well, we appreciate you taking time to tell about the Marine Corps' newest operation. And we certainly hope your project is successful. And I might add that Sgt. Gilliam's job is as dangerous as a lineman—as that's where he is—right up on the front lines with his Psychological Warfare weapon. And indeed, it is a weapon. This is Marine Radio Correspondent Dick Hill, with Sgt. Ward Gilliam, from Richmond, Virginia, returning you to the *Marine Corps Show* in Hollywood, California.

Sgt. Ward Gilliam, in G-2, was a pioneer user of the Marine Corps' newest weapon—PSYWAR. Since that broadcast in January 1953, it has grown in importance in all the military services. This mode of operation is not decisive by itself, but in combination with conventional combat weapons, Psychological Warfare contributes materially to the winning of wars.

Precious Medal: The author and thousands of Korean War Veterans received this 50th Anniversary Medal from Kim Dae-jung, the President of the Republic of Korea. It was awarded 50 years to the day from the outbreak of the war, June 25, 2000. (Author's Collection)

Chosin Reservoir Marines on the rim of the plateau on their long, bitter-cold walk to safety. David Douglas Duncan, photographer, describes the historic moment: "They started down the narrow, tortuous road winding to the canyon below. They walked with necks bent, shoulders hunched up, eyes almost closed to a kind of cold against which there was no protection ... in which no clothes had warmth. So they just walked ... carried their rifles ... and froze." (Photography Collection, Harry Ransom-Humanities Reseach Center, The University of Texas at Austin)

11

THE RED TIDE

As I learned in the business world, failing to listen to major concerns can be costly. In the military, it can cost lives. And it did in Korea. The Communist Red Chinese Army entered the Korean War to help their North Korean allies. But it was not supposed to happen. At least that's what General Douglas MacArthur, Commander in Chief, United Nations Command, had said. And this was despite the red flag intelligence reports that crossed his desk, suggesting the Chinese were close to crossing into Korea.

In November of 1950, Chinese soldiers started trickling over the Manchurian border. Soon, that trickle swelled to 120,000 troops, then became a flood of 780,000. The Chinese supplied the two essentials the North Koreans desperately needed: experienced troops and arms. The Red Tide of enemy troops changed the dynamics of the Korean War and dragged it out for another two years. And the Red Tide also dragged me and thousands of others into service.

The force of the Red Tide was like a giant tsunami headed straight for the UN forces and the U.S. Marines at the Chosin Reservoir in the far northeastern part of North Korea. I had not arrived yet, but a fellow combat correspondent, Frank Kerr, was there. He was Sgt. Frank Kerr then, a young, good-looking 20-year-old Marine Combat photographer. He is one of the few living Marines to have seen, fought, photographed, and written about the very first Red Tide. Kerr was eyewitness to the November–December 1950 Chosin Reservoir battle that combatants describe as hell itself. In the North Korean mountains near Manchuria, in the dead of winter, about 15,000 weary, allied ground troops—mostly elements of the First Marine Division and a regimental combat team of the U.S. Army's Seventh Infantry Division—faced 120,000 fresh Chinese troops. We later learned that the enemy had been ordered to annihilate our allied troops "to the last man."

THE CHOSIN FEW

The Chosin Reservoir battle goes down as one of the most savage in history. The survivors have stuck together all these years with their exclusive group—The Chosin Few Association -Korea 1950.

The gooks, as the leathernecks called the Chinese, almost succeeded in their mission. The 15,000 allies suffered 12,000 casualties, including more than 3,000 KIA's (Killed in Action) and 6,000 WIA's (Wounded in Action). Thousands more suffered severe frostbite from the frigid temperatures—minus 30 degrees—and the god-awful northern winds blowing from Siberia and Manchuria. No wonder our guys called the winter "Korea's second enemy." The battle was tougher than the Chinese thought it was going to be. They had 43,500 casualties, including 28,000 KIA's and 15,000 WIA's. The Chosin Reservoir battle was their first bloody nose in the Korean War.

Historians describe Chosin as the most savage battle of modern warfare, comparable to Tarawa, the bloodiest battle of World War II. The press likened Chosin to the Alamo or Custer's Last Stand because of the seemingly hopeless odds. *Time* magazine described it as "unparalleled in U.S. military history. An epic of great suffering and great valor." President Ronald Reagan in his first inaugural address cited Chosin as among the epics of military history. Survivors emerged from the ordeal with a Presidential Unit Citation for "decisively defeating seven enemy divisions, together with elements of three others." Chosin has been immortalized in the movie, *Retreat, Hell!* starring Frank Lovejoy, Richard Carlson, Russ Tamblyn, and Anita Louise. Major General Oliver P. Smith, commanding general of the First Marine Division, when asked if his men were retreating, uttered the words that became a battle cry around the world: *"Retreat, hell! We're just attacking in a different direction."*

Frank Kerr also saw a "Christmas Miracle." The Chosin fighters, by checkmating the Chinese forces in the mountains, enabled the evacuation of 100,000 North Koreans—that's right, *North* Koreans, not South Koreans—men, women, and children by sea. It was Christmas Eve, 1950. The U.S. government formally termed the humanitarian feat "the greatest rescue operation in the history of mankind." Never in recorded history have combatants rescued so many enemy civilians in the midst of battle. Those refugees are now living free, many in America.

In 1983, Frank Kerr helped found one of the military's most unique associations, The Chosin Few of Korea. The name stems from the fact that so few survived the battle. The association's goal is to unite the survivors of the Chosin Reservoir campaign into one body of sharing, caring companionship and everlasting remembrance of those who did not survive. The association has 3,917 active members from all U.S. Services, plus former members of the Republic of Korea (ROK, South Korean) forces, British Marine Commandos, and Royal Australian Air Force members.

Among the countless articles written about the Chosin Reservoir battle, this descriptive account from Frank Kerr is one of the best. It appeared in *Leatherneck*, December 1990:

Maggie Higgins, face covered with mud, finishes a story for the New York Herald Tribune. *She was with the Marines during their "advance to the rear," the road back from the Chosin Reservoir in December 1950. (Photo Courtesy Doubleday and Company)*

Former Marine combat photographer, Frank Kerr, is co-founder of the world famous Chosin Few Association. Kerr played a dual role in Korea. Besides shooting award-winning photos, he was a valued rifleman in the battles at Pusan, Inchon and Chosin Reservoir. (Photo Courtesy Frank Kerr)

The RESERVOIR

The battle at the Chosin Reservoir in 1950 has since become the stuff of legend and doctrine. Armies the world over study it as a classic of warfare, especially small-unit actions. *Time* magazine termed it "unparalleled in U.S. military history...an epic of great suffering and great valor." President Ronald Reagan cited it in his first inaugural address.

Chosin pitted roughly 15,000 allied ground troops—mostly elements of the First Marine Division, along with a regimental combat team of the Army's Seventh Infantry Division, a small unit of British Royal Marine Commandos and South Korean troops—against some 120,000 Chinese. "Annihilate the American Marines to the last man," were their orders, presumably to send psychological shockwaves through other allied forces.

Official records place Marine Corps casualties at more than 11,000. Survivors have since researched and calculated that the combined allied troops suffered roughly 12,000 casualties, including 3,000 killed, 6,000 wounded, plus thousands of severe frostbite cases from the minus-30 degree temperature. The Chinese had an estimated 43,500 casualties, including 28,000 killed.

Historians label Chosin as the most savage battle of modern warfare in ratio of casualties to the men engaged. The Chosin Marines emerged from their ordeal with a Presidential Unit Citation for "decisively defeating seven entire divisions, together with elements of three others." Another indicator of the ferocity is that seventeen Medals of Honor were awarded for the fighting.

As the battle unfolded against seemingly hopeless odds, the armchair experts wrote off the Marines as a "lost legion," doomed for extinction, victims of another heroic but tragic Alamo or Custer's Last Stand. Again, dead wrong. The Marines didn't get the word that their cause was hopeless.

Legendary Lewis B. "Chesty" Puller, then a regimental commander, struck a key to the outcome while reflecting after the war. He said that the First Marines Division at Chosin was the finest fighting force ever fielded by the United States.

If the Chosin Marines were not the best, they certainly must rank near the top. They were lean, mean and combat-sharp as they entered those mountains. Their leadership, from NCOs to the highest-ranking officers, was superb. And if the Corps' philosophy of "every man a rifleman first and foremost" ever needed validation, the Reservoir surely provided it.

When the Chinese sprung their carefully laid trap, planning to divide, conquer and annihilate, they caught the proverbial tiger by the tail. And they got mauled.

Even before the battle, the Marines captured a sprinkling of Chinese, but their warnings of a new enemy fell on deaf ears at General MacArthur's headquarters in Tokyo. Then, on November 1, the Seventh Marine Regiment met and clobbered a Chinese division in the foothills of the mountains. The enemy pulled back and vanished, and we followed slowly.

The hero's hero of the campaign has to be Major General Oliver P. Smith, commander of the First Division. He advanced cautiously, probing the strength of the new enemy, establishing rearguard strongholds of supply and defense, all despite the Army command's exhortations to race blindly into the unknown. And,

BULLSEYE FOR M1

General George Patton called the M1 rifle the greatest battle implement ever devised.

of course, he led us out under the banner of his immortal battle cry, "Retreat, Hell! We're just attacking in a different direction." Eyewitnesses confirm he said exactly that, but some stateside skeptics, never close to the battleground, let alone the general, claim he would never utter such language.

By November 27, the Fifth and Seventh Marine Regiments had advanced to a village named Yudam-ni on the western side of the frozen reservoir. Over the mountains behind us, other units were digging in at Hagaru-ri at the bottom end of the reservoir and farther south at Koto-ri. That night, everything hit the fan, everywhere. From then on, we were either closely engaged with the Chinese, often at bayonet and grenade range, or eyeing each other like killer wolves seeking a lethal edge.

It's an experience to see literal hordes of the enemy rushing toward you or to glare at him so close you can smell him, or have him leap, over your head, or to reload before he does. But it was not all fury.

China hands among the Division answered the Chinese curse in their own language and added zingers of their own for good measure. They even captured a former Chinese houseboy, greeting him like the long-lost friend he was. Above all, though, was the deepening of our undying admiration and respect for Navy corpsmen and Marine pilots. They're a special breed and any ground-type who's heard shots fired in anger places them on a pedestal of honor.

It was at Yudam-ni that I again screwed up in my "secondary" job—but intentionally. The morning after the initial Chinese assaults, I came across a badly wounded platoon sergeant slumped in grief at the loss of friends. His parka was covered with frost, and his haggard face was a mask of ice and coagulated blood. To this day, I know he would have been the greatest picture of the war. To this day I'm glad I did not intrude on his privacy.

His face said everything about the suffering at Chosin, especially the cold. Reams have been written and movies made about the battle, but no one has ever captured that savage, mind-numbing, flesh-killing cold. It was minus-30 degrees and below, lashed by Manchurian winds that would burst thermometers by today's wind-chill factors. It's unbelievable that anyone could survive such temperatures, let alone move and fight. Hell did indeed freeze over once upon a time—and we were there.

The cold froze weapons and men alike. My carbine, which had a nasty habit of jamming at all the wrong times down south, flat-out refused to budge at Chosin. So I tossed it for a trusty M1 rifle. It would only fire a round by hand-operated bold action. My "secondary weapon," my camera, performed flawlessly, however. But I had to conserve film because I was running low.

Esprit de corps, discipline, resolve and devotion to the Corps and each other enabled us to prevail at the Reservoir. And it may be hard to believe, when ordered to start back, the battle-weary Marines openly worried, not about the Chinese everywhere we looked, but about how other Marines would view our withdrawal. It mattered not that the U.S. Eighth Army had collapsed on the far side of the peninsula, leaving us alone in far northern Korea, or that any farther advance would be pointless as well as suicidal. After all, the tradition of the Corps rode on our shoulders then and there, and we were truly concerned that we might tarnish it.

Unabashed pride of the Corps was demonstrated repeatedly at Chosin. When the Yudam-ni Marines fought back to Hagaru-ri, they formed ranks, with-

SEMPER FIVE?

When e-mailing fellow Marines, I sign off with "Semper Fi." A young grandson of one of my friends saw this and added his own personal touch. He greets his buddies with a high-five salute and says: "Semper Five!"

out orders given, and marched into the perimeter to greetings of tears and the exaltation, "Look at those bastards, those magnificent bastards." The touching moment was repeated at Koto-ri several days later. From Medal of Honor recipients to a future Commandant to everyday infantrymen, all have said or written that their first sight of the battered but defiant Division misted their eyes and choke their throats.

The final phase of the historic breakout began December 9 with the Marines striking south from Koto-ri and fighting down and out of the mountains of the frozen Chosin. Then, they were sea-lifted to South Korea to be rested and refitted for battles yet to come. And so another glorious chapter was written into the distinguished history of the United States Marine Corps.

When I arrived a year and a half after the historic Chosin battle, the war had become a static contest for position and terrain. Some named it "the battle for the hills." Lee Ballenger, who served in the Marines, probably nailed it best by calling it "The Outpost War," after his best-selling book. Yet the war remained bloody and costly. Marines suffered more than 40 percent of their casualties during battles along the MLR (Main Line of Resistance). The Red Chinese continued their "Red Tide" attacks, pouring over the hills we called Bunker, Carson, Detroit, Frisco, Hook, Vegas, Ungok, and Warsaw. The Chinese charged in massed human waves of 50 to 100. The bugle-blowing Red Chinese tried not only to breach defenses, but also to intimidate the highly outnumbered Marines. They would break through our lines occasionally, and even take some of the hills for a day or two, then we would get them back. However, not even their eerie, headache-causing bugle blowing could intimidate the Marine Corps' First Marine Division.

While Marines bring in a wounded man on a stretcher, combat correspondents TSgt. Jim Coleman (left) and MSgt. Jim Galloway catch their breath before filing their Siberia Hill firefight story. Photo taken August 9, 1952, close to Chang-Dan, Korea. (Marine Corps Photo/Sgt. Edward Scullin)

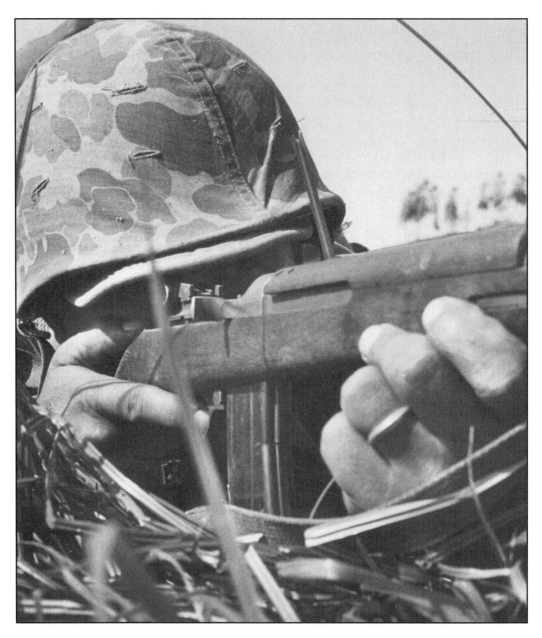

A Marine takes aim and prepares to fire at his target, as recorded by David Douglas Duncan in Korea, 1950. Thanks to the skill of riflemen like these, the Main Line of Resistance (MLR) was in good hands. (Photography Collection, Harry Ransom-Humanities Research Center, The University of Texas at Austin)

12

DEFENDING THE MLR

The Marines fought two wars in Korea. The first, a "traditional" war from 1950–1951, witnessed the Marines assault a target, take it, and move on to the next objective. These were the tactics employed at Pusan, Inchon, and Chosin. The second war, the stalemate phase of the war from 1952–1953, became an "outpost war," as Lee Ballenger called it in his bestseller, *The Outpost War.* This was bloody, frustrating, static warfare. Over 7,500 Marines became casualties during this period, when an arbitrary line drawn in the hills became the Main Line of Resistance (MLR).

The Main Line of Resistance was the first thing that many civilian reporters wanted to see in the Marines' sector. It was an important position opposite the better trained and equipped Chinese Communists, not opposite the North Korean Army. Some reporters that I escorted there to view it were surprised. They expected something like the Great Wall of China, something that would offer better protection for our troops. Instead, the MLR was a wide-open line of trenches and bunkers running for 20 miles or so, twisting and turning over hills and ridges. The MLR sat close to the 38th Parallel, smack dab where the war had started on June 25, 1950. The United Nations' forces had not gained an inch in territory. It would remain that way until the war's end in July 1953.

By agreement between the United Nations and North Korea, the war became a "static war" as the peace negotiations continued at nearby Panmunjom. Unlike the earlier battles at Pusan, Inchon, and Chosin, the two armies in 1952–1953 stood and faced each other at the line drawn in the hilly Korean soil. Marines were not used to fighting this way. It was a whole new ballgame. A fellow Marine in Korea about the same time I was, Lee Ballenger, explained the new fighting conditions in his bestselling book, *The Outpost War:*

Fighting a static war was a new role for the Marine Corps. It wasn't their favorite maneuver.

The U.S. Marine Corps' traditional role is to attack an entrenched enemy, seize his ground for mop-up and occupation forces, and move on to the next unlucky target. Midway through the Korean War, however, the Marines were forced to abandon their usual tactics to fight a limited war.

The Marines were organized and trained as light infantry to hit hard and to maneuver swiftly. The idea of digging in and fighting defensively for any great length of time was foreign to Marine thinking and training. Siege warfare was the antithesis of Marine Corps philosophy. Creation of a military stalemate during the last half of the Korean War, however, found the Marines in precisely that position. Consequently, they had to improvise, to create tactics, and to improve methods with which they had little experience. Outpost warfare was not a planned tactic; it just evolved by the blood of some thirteen thousand young men. Painfully and slowly, the Marines learned from trial and error that a static war could be as deadly as one of maneuver. It simply took longer. Functioning in slow motion, it was a war of attrition against the largest army in the world.

Shades of David and Goliath? The United Nations forces were fighting the largest army in the world: 780,000 Chinese (30 divisions) and another 250,000 North Koreans (10 divisions). The UN forces comprised five American divisions, a British Commonwealth division, and a few brigades and regiments of Greeks, Turks, French, Australians, and others, as well as the Republic of Korea (ROK) Army.

During my tour in 1952–1953, the First Marine Division was toe-to-toe with the Communist Chinese on the MLR. Our right flank was on the Sea of Japan. Our left flank was linked with the South Korean ROKs. The Marines' three rifle regiments—the First, Fifth and Seventh—were spread out thinly across 20 miles of high ridges along the coastal range. In all, the Marines had 27 rifle companies defending the MLR. Directly supporting the Marines were the Eleventh Artillery Regiment, First Marine Air Wing, the division's Reconnaissance Company, First Tank Battalion, and occasional naval support, as well as the bread-and-butter support from the other units in the division's table of organization and equipment (TO&E).

A soldier really earned his combat pay when he passed the MLR to enter no-man's-land. Each Marine earned an extra $45 each month for serving in a combat zone. Regular military pay was $75 per month.

Lacking in numbers, but never in fighting spirit, the Marines valiantly defended their sector of the MLR. The following brief story by Lane Phalen, appearing at www.medalofhonor.com, illustrates this fighting valor:

Putting His Men First: *A Young Marine Leader Provides the Spark to Recapture Lost Ground*

George H. O'Brien, Jr., makes it clear: "This Medal of Honor is not mine. I hold it in trust for so many young people who didn't become grandfathers."

Nominated for the medal by many of his men, O'Brien received it for his actions during a battle on October 27, 1952. A second lieutenant at the time, he was a platoon leader with the Marine Corps Reserve, Company H, 3rd Battalion, 7th Marines, 1st Marine Division (Reinforced).

Suddenly, he and his men found themselves coming under an intense mortar and artillery bombardment while preparing to assault a vitally important hill position on the main line of resistance (MLR). The enemy, with a numerically superior force, had overrun the MLR the night before.

When the attack signal was given, O'Brien leaped from his trench, shouting for his men to follow. Exposed to enemy fire, he ran across and up the enemy-held hill through a hail of deadly small-arms, artillery and mortar fire. Shot in the arm, the Fort Worth, Texas, native continued to crawl near the well-entrenched enemy position. He stood and waved his men onward, pausing just long enough to help a wounded Marine.

Closing on the enemy, O'Brien used hand grenades and his carbine with deadly effectiveness, killing at least three of them. Wounded himself by grenades on three occasions, he refused to be evacuated for medical treatment. His platoon was his main concern. For nearly four hours, O'Brien continued to lead and encourage his men.

When the attack finally halted, he quickly set up a defense with his remaining men, and prepared for a counterattack, all the while tending to the wounded and expediting their evacuation. Relief troops arrived to man the position, but O'Brien remained to cover the evacuation to ensure no wounded were left behind. A constant source of inspiration to all who observed him, O'Brien was instrumental in the recapture of a strategic position on the MLR.

Though not a POW himself, O'Brien accompanied the first American POWs to return to the United States. On the trip, he interrogated returning Marines. After getting home, he sought to return to the life he had left and set up a business he still works today. O'Brien enjoys his growing family that includes 13 grandchildren. Reflecting back, he said: "The Lord has been awfully good to me."

––––––––––––––

Since Lane Phalen's story appeared, Congressional Medal of Honor Recipient, 2nd Lt. George Herman O'Brien Jr., USMC, died March 13, 2005, in Midland, Texas. He was 78. Of the approximately 3,400 recipi-

Marine mortar crewmen blast the enemy with accuracy and teamwork. Mortars, on both sides of the front line, were a key weapon in the Korean War. (Marine Corps Photo/Sgt. Frank Kerr)

ents of the Medal of Honor, which was established in 1862, roughly 130 are still living.

To keep track of the enemy, Marines set up outposts and listening posts on high ground or ridges. Marines would dig trenches and, where possible, construct bunkers for protection. Usually a squad of 13 men would man these outposts, but when necessary, a full platoon would maintain the positions. I saw the Chinese use about every weapon conceivable to try to move the Marines off their outposts: burp guns, Tommy guns, pistols, hand grenades, mortar and artillery fire, machine guns, bayonets, knives, and even fists, feet, and teeth during hand-to-hand combat. They wanted these key positions as much as we did.

Another "weapon" of sorts was the Chinese bugle, played on the battlefield as a communication device over small distances. The enemy would signal troop movements with a short bugle tattoo and charge to a wild and rousing blast. The enemy would also occasionally try to confuse us by blowing charge signals without charging. The brass sound could rattle the nerves of veterans and newcomers. The Chinese bugle became a sought-after souvenir.

One of the landmarks close to the MLR was the picturesque Imjin River. A tributary of the Han River, the Imjin flowed in a meandering course close to our First Marine PIO Headquarters, where I worked.

"Don't let the calmness of the river fool you," MSgt. Bob Fugate pointed out. "During the monsoons in July and August, the Imjin becomes a raging torrent."

Imjin means "water dragon," a very apt name for the river during monsoon season. It reminded me of the Mississippi River that separates my hometown of Minneapolis and our Twin City neighbor to the east, Saint Paul. However, the Imjin is just a creek compared to our broad, powerful Mississippi River that flows and snakes several thousand miles from northern Minnesota to the Gulf of Mexico.

Early in the war lots of blood from both sides was spilled in the Imjin River. One of our UN allies, the British Gloucestershire Regiment, engaged the Communist Chinese in the Battle of the Imjin River occurring north of the MLR at the double bend of the Imjin. Despite being outnumbered, the Brits held off the Chinese.

Many of my recording memories are with the Seventh Regiment, a proud unit. Here is a brief salute to Able Company, First Battalion, Seventh Marine Regiment, by one of its former members, Sgt. Major J. R. Skinner, USMC (retired):

During the monsoons in summer, the Imjin River becomes a raging torrent. Blood from both sides was spilled in this tributary of the Han River. (Author's Collection)

Able Company, 1st Battalion, 7th Regiment, 1st Marine Division, Fleet Marine Force, is only one of 27 rifle companies of the 1st Marine Division. Probably no better nor worse than any other rifle company in the Division, but "Stable Able" is "MY" company and I am quite proud of its accomplishments. I was so very proud to say many times: "Stable Able! Saddle up! Move it out!" We had prior World War II "China Hands" who knew all the skills of war-fighting. Also island-hopping veterans of WWII who know well the art of combat. And fuzzy-cheeked youngsters who learned how to load and fire the M1 rifle off the fantail of the troop transport en route to Korea. We had high school and college grads, high school drop-outs, etc. The bulk of the company were Marine Corps Reserves recalled to active duty leaving families, jobs, businesses, colleges and just getting settled in their civilian pursuits after World War II. We were a hodge-podge of American society. And "Stable Able" was bonded into a "Brotherhood" that can only be accomplished by Down and Dirty Combat. And I wish to salute our Fallen Brothers—and remember them as

A three-man team of Marines in position atop a hill overlooking their target, September 1950. (Photography Collection, Harry Ransom-Humanities Center, The University of Texas at Austin)

the healthy young men that loved and were loved. They are our "Brothers."

Semper Fidelis

Sergeant Major J.R. Skinner, USMC (Retired)

This is the same "Stable Able" group in which Francis "Bud" Grunert served. I recall Grunert telling me "all hell broke loose" along the ridge on the day of his capture. Here is the Seventh Regiment's Command Diary describing the heavy action from October 26–November 1, 1952. This secret information is now declassified and open information to the public:

SEVENTH REGIMENT COMMAND DIARY

Summary of Action: 26 OCT–1 NOV 1952

Battle for the Hook

For approximately one week, the MLR in the "Hook" area, and outposts Warsaw and Ronson, were subjected to intense accurate shelling of all calibers. Bunkers and entrenchments suffered heavy damage, but were restored nightly by Marines and 200 KSC's.

At 1830 on 26 Oct the enemy forced the outpost at Ronson to withdraw to the MLR. At 1900 the main attack engaged the MLR at the "Hook." At 2030 the enemy succeeded in penetrating the Hook area. By 2200, the penetration had been contained, though heavy fighting continued. One battalion (3/1), Division reserve regiment was moved into an assembly area behind the 7th Marines, on the MLR. At 2250 "A" Co 1/7 counterattacked.

Marines busy reinforcing their outpost. (Sketch by John Chalk, Leatherneck *magazine)*

How Company 3/7 commenced counterattacking from the right flank at 0440, and advanced slowly against extremely heavy resistance in coordination with "Able" Company. At 0930 both companies were engaged in hand-to-hand fight on the slopes of the "Hook." [This is when Sgt. Francis Grunert was captured.] The fight continued sporadically until 0600 on the morning of 28 October. Friendly casualties totaled 70 KIA, 386 WIA and 39 missing. The great majority of these casualties were incurred as a result of artillery and mortar fire. Enemy losses are estimated at 532 KIA and 216 WIA. Air strikes during 27–28 October totaled 260 sorties. Both air and artillery were highly effective. The enemy attack was supported by an estimated 17,000 rounds of artillery.

The Seventh Regiment's Command Diary for November 1952 contains the following passage describing how the enemy pressure continued on the MLR. The replacements joining the Seventh Regiment included Navy corpsmen to care for the wounded for Marines:

From: Commanding Officer

To: Commandant of the Marine Corps

Subj: Command Diary for period 1–30 November, 1952

1. SUMMARY

> a. The 7th Marine Regiment was in contact with the enemy during the period of 1–16 November. Opposing enemy forces consisted of elements of the 118th and 119th Divisions of the 40th CCF (Chinese Communist Forces)

Army. The enemy continued his active defense of the area. Construction and improvement of tunnel type emplacements, personnel shelters and communication-supply trenchlines were noted, particularly in enemy forward areas. Small probes, ambushing of friendly patrols and minor attacks characterized enemy activity. A total of 1,593 rounds of mixed artillery and mortar fell in the 7th Marine sector.

A wounded rifleman is pulled off the line by a fellow Marine. (Sketch by John Chalk, Leatherneck *magazine)*

b. During the period of 1–16 November 1952, the 7th Marine Regiment was assigned the mission of occupying, defending, and continuing improvement of the MLR, Line Jamestown. All three battalions were initially on line with the 2nd on the left and the 1st on the right. At 0323, the right battalion was relieved on position by elements of the 1st Commonwealth (British) Division and the regimental boundary was adjusted accordingly.

On 8 November, 1952, an air draft of 17 USN enlisted corpsmen was received and on 9 November, a surface draft of 23 USMC officers, 404 USMC enlisted and 38 USN enlisted corpsmen was received. Both of these drafts received a five (5) day period of indoctrination training prior to assignment to respective units.

Mail was received and distributed. The regimental newspaper *The Ridgerunner* was published and distributed daily. Daily briefings were held while the regiment was on the line and as necessary in reserve.

The first replacement corpsmen—17 of them—were flown in because they were needed fast. Without regard for their own personal safety, Navy corpsmen saved many a Marine on the battlefield in Korea.

Corpsmen were highly respected and a part of the Marine Corps' family.

Going back to reserve was like a vacation for linemen. Hot chow and a shower was something to write home about.

James Brady served in Korea, commanded a Marine rifle platoon, and was awarded the Bronze Star for valor. He wrote *The Scariest Place in the World* and other top sellers. In *The Coldest War*, he wrote something that most Marines in a rifle company had probably thought about often: "When you weren't fighting, the war was pretty good."

When you were not fighting, you were off the MLR and safely back in battalion reserve. You could relax and breathe a little easier. Much of the stress disappeared, for awhile. You felt like a human being. You got little things like a hot shower, clean clothes, hot chow, extra rack time, and even sports. You could play volleyball, pass a football around, or play catch with a baseball. And there was mail call. After catching up on the homefront you had a chance to write home. If you were real lucky, and the stars were just right, there could be a USO show. Maybe you would see headliners like Bob Hope, Francis Langford, Jack Benny, Al Jolson, Debbie Reynolds, Mickey Rooney, or Danny Kaye. Regardless of the star status, all USO performers in Korea were the greatest. Movies were also a big event in reserve, especially one starring John Wayne or Marilyn Monroe. Being back in reserve meant getting updated on news and listening to music on Armed Forces Radio. Some of the guys got caught up on their latest Mike Hammer thriller by Mickey Spillane. Or they started a card game.

Not all the time was spent on fun and games, however. There was also training and guard duty, but no one minded. You were off the line. One Pfc. rifleman explained during a radio interview about being in battalion reserve:

> For me, being in reserve is a little like a mini-R&R. (Rest and Recuperation.) But you've got to savor it, because it goes real fast. After a few days you're back up there. Back in the bunker or out on patrol. But that's what your job is—to defend the MLR.

A Marine Tank, First Tank Battallion, in a road block just west of Div. Command Post at Masan, Korea, 1950. Same type used in Operation Echo when the author participated in a diversionary tactic against the Chinese. (Marine Corps Photo/TSgt. Helms)

13
OPERATION ECHO

I doubt if my official military records show it, but I worked with G-2 (the intelligence people) on a top-secret project. The information is now declassified.

Operation Echo took place in December of 1952. I was ordered to see the commanding officer at G-2, a short walk from my PIO tent. I knew the clerk by sight and he smiled and ushered me in. It was obvious that he knew what all this was about.

"Corporal Hill?" the captain asked. "At ease."

"Yes, sir," I confirmed.

"You use a tape recorder quite a bit, don't you?"

"Yes, sir. I work with one everyday."

"Good," he returned. "What we're talking about is secret. Top secret. I don't want this going any further. Understand?"

"Yes, sir." I was beginning to sound like a "yes" man. But that's how it is between officers and enlisted men.

He explained that Operation Echo was a diversionary tactic to make the Communist Chinese believe that they heard moving tanks. Our officers were betting that the enemy would react by launching an artillery barrage against the "attacking tanks." The captain wondered if it were possible to record the sound of a moving tank, then play that sound back amplified over loud speakers. Neat idea on G-2's part. For most of the last half of the war, tanks sat in stationary positions behind

TANK POWER

Military historians praise the role of tanks in the Korean War. The tankers— the men inside—provided much of the support fire the rifle companies needed.

the MLR and provided support fire for ground operations, but the tanks did move around to gain better positions.

Before meeting at the First Tank Battalion the next morning, I did some homework on Marine tanks. My key source was MSgt. Bob Fugate, combat correspondent extraordinaire. Marine armor, I learned, played an important role in Korea. Marine M26 Pershing tanks were equipped to fight enemy armor, and played key roles in all Korean campaigns, including the battles of Pusan, Inchon, Seoul, and the Chosin Reservoir. The tankers faced immense challenges. Difficult movement in the trench-riddled, battle-scarred, ruggedly hilly terrain was compounded by the arctic weather conditions. Since the tanks only had steel tracks without rubber pads, tank crews felt as though they were riding on ice skates. Those that were there said it took a lot of courage for drivers to stay with their tanks and drive them. Tankers were gutsy guys.

As instructed, I reported to the First Tank Battalion at 0900 the next morning. In my jeep I had my tape-recording equipment and plenty of 3M reel-to-reel tape. A MSgt. tanker, seeing me drive in, waved me toward their headquarters bunker. This bunker was the fanciest I had ever seen. The Hilton hotel chain could get room-decorating ideas from this one. Most bunker bulkheads were just plain sandbags. This one had blankets over them to add a homey touch. In the middle of the plush bunker were two blazing Yukon oil stoves. Some of the bunkers did not rate one stove. Close by was their war table with two telephones surrounded by detailed maps. I wondered for an instant

MARINE CORRESPONDENT

The author's badge that permitted carte blanche travel for combat correspondents in Korea. A collector's item, it is believed to be the only one in existence. (Author's Collection)

what was different about the table. Then it hit me. A cloth was draped over it. Yet what really convinced me that Marine tankers lived like kings was the coffee I was served by a Pfc. This was not the C-ration instant coffee I was used to. As I was sipping it to melt away Korea's freeze, I asked the sergeant, "Real coffee beans?"

"Real Kona blend coffee beans, right from Hawaii," the MSgt. beamed.

Impressed, I asked how you could find coffee like that in Korea.

"I was stationed at Pearl Harbor for a while. I got used to Kona coffee. So some of my buddies who are still there send it to me. I'm running low on it. Better let 'em know."

It must be nice to have friends in all the right places, but when you are a master sergeant, you can do anything. Wow! Two Yukon stoves and Kona coffee. I guessed he experienced World War II and now was serving in Korea. He earned it, I was sure.

That was the end of our socializing. We spent the rest of the morning setting up my equipment and recording two M46 tanks. Nothing is more distinctive than the squeaking steel tracks on a tank. It took an hour to get what I wanted. We were anxious to try it out.

CONFUSED ENEMY

Our little tank tactic worked like a charm. The Chinese thought they heard real tanks.

Two nights later, at 2300 on a moonless night, my tape recorder and two huge loudspeakers were strategically placed in a snow-covered ravine close to the Seventh Regiment's position on the MLR. When instructed, I turned on the tape player. Jesus! It was exhilarating. The sound of moving tanks came amplified through the 20-inch speakers. A lot was riding on this little maneuver. A reconnaissance squad 1,000 yards east was getting ready to jump off from the MLR and scout the enemy's strength. The Chinese took the bait by launching a salvo at the tank sounds, thinking they had an easy target. One officer, phone clutched in his hand, put the word through to the recon squad leader.

"This is Echo man. Go ahead. Good luck," he signaled.

The shelling continued as the recording of moving tanks played on. They sent in round after round of mortar and artillery fire. The Marines respected their accuracy. Operation Echo continued for some 30 minutes. The diversionary tactic bought time for the men from the Seventh Regiment to successfully complete their recon mission. Undetected, the black-faced squad determined the positions and strength of the enemy.

The next day back at division headquarters, MSgt. H.B. Wells said, "I heard you're assigned part-time to Intelligence now, Hill."

H.B. was fishing for a reaction, but the assignment was supposed to be secret. How did he hear about it? Hell, he was a master sergeant. Master sergeants know everything, especially the top-secret stuff.

The United States Marine Corps Combat Correspondents Association logo. The USMCCCA is the only organization of its kind in the U.S. military services. (Photo Courtesy USMCCCA)

Marines charging toward enemy guns without even a downward glance as they sloshed over an enemy body. Again, D.D.D. makes combat photography look easy. (Photography Collection, Harry Ransom-Humanities Research Center, The University of Texas at Austin)

14

THE GROUND POUNDERS

Korea was a ground pounders' war. Rifle platoons held the day-to-day responsibility for keeping the enemy away from the Main Line of Resistance.

Members of rifle platoons are dedicated, disciplined, and skilled warriors. Marine ground pounders, or infantrymen, have the best officers—commissioned and non-commissioned—in the military leading them. Their primary weapon in Korea was the M1 Garand Rifle. Its effective firing range was 440 yards. One old salt from World War II in the Seventh Regiment, during a radio interview, told me that General George Patton called the M1 "the greatest battle implement ever devised."

Marines are well trained as soldiers and problem solvers. If a buddy goes down, any Marine can effectively take over a Browning Automatic Rifle (BAR) or man a machine gun. They are formidable with fixed bayonets, fearsome in hand-to-hand combat, and deadly accurate with hand grenades.

Each time I interviewed one of our troops, I came away with more respect and a new friend. Consider Cpl. Lester E. Little of Phillipsburg, New Jersey. He was a BAR man. He volunteered to be on the line with the Seventh Regiment. Little was a sole surviving son. He lost his father, also a Marine, on Iwo Jima, and lost two brothers who served in the Army in Europe during World War II. When I met him in December 1952, he was getting ready to go home with two Purple Hearts on his chest. Little was a ground pounder and proud of it. (See the chapter entitled *Saving Corporal Little*.)

Ground pounders, or grunts, as they're affectionately called, have been around since Alexander the Great in 300 BC. Alexander, called the greatest general in history, wisely surrounded himself with infantry soldiers. He conquered the Persian

Empire with thousands of superior foot soldiers at his command.

The public has always pulled for the infantry. They're the mud-rain-frost-and-wind boys. They win the wars.

Ernie Pyle, the famous World War II correspondent, was close to the infantry and told their stories in newspapers. He spoke for the "GI Joe" in all the services. Pyle could have easily been describing Alexander the Great's army in Persia, General Eisenhower's in Europe, or the Marines in Korea when he wrote:

> I love the infantry because they are the underdogs. They are the mud-rain-frost-and-wind boys. They have no comforts and even learn to live without the necessities. And in the end they are the guys that wars can't be won without.

The Marine Corps started out with two battalions of foot soldiers. That was in 1775 during the Revolutionary War. Now, as then, the Corps has always been structured around a core of infantry. In the Korean War, the First Marine Division had three infantry regiments, plus plenty of firepower to support the ground troops. This support included air, artillery, tank, and reconnaissance units. Yet the rifle platoon was the backbone of the Marines in Korea. James Brady, a Korean War Marine, tells how these platoons were structured in this excerpt from his best-selling book, *The Coldest War:*

> A Marine rifle platoon in Korea was a superbly balanced tactical unit with enormous firepower and an eminently sensible fundamental premise: in combat no one man can reasonably be expected to control directly and effectively more than three other men. In a firefight, you can't keep tabs on more than the three Marines and still be aware of the enemy. A Marine rifle platoon has three squads whose squad leaders are

172

trained to maintain contact with the platoon leader. He issues orders not to forty men, but only to these three sergeants. In their turn, they each control three fire teams, each of which is commanded by a corporal fire team leader. They look to the squad leader for orders, he to them for action. In the fire team the corporal has three men, whom he controls and who look always to him during a firefight.

Marines scale the breakwater that surrounds Inchon during their surprise invasion, September 15, 1950. (Photo Courtesy Doubleday and Company)

Army platoons also have three squads, but the squads aren't broken down into fire teams, but remain an unwieldy straggle of ten or a dozen men. There is one other material distinction between Marine and Army rifle platoons: fire power and the Browning Automatic Rifle. The BAR is a wonderfully steady, fast-firing, very accurate weapon. Each Marine fire team is built around the BAR. A Marine platoon had nine BARs, the Army platoon only three, one to each squad.

The BAR weighed twenty pounds even without ammo, and the ammo belts weighed that much again, yet it seemed that a stunted little guy weighing about 130 pounds was always lugging it. At Quantico we bitched about being chosen as BAR men during field problems. Out here you couldn't pry one away from a BAR man. It was the finest one-man weapon employed in the infantry, a great weapon. It had a range with a certain type of ball cartridge of 5,500 yards— more than three miles. BAR men were forever arguing over that, whether you could hit a man at three miles, or if at that distance he had disappeared below the curvature of the earth and you couldn't even see him. Marines delighted in intellectual debates like that, loud and obscene.

One of the strengths of the Marine Corps is its unity. Every Marine is a rifleman first. Regardless of job or rank, every Marine may become a ground pounder. Fellow combat correspondent Frank Kerr filled in as a combat Marine in the Fifth Regiment in the early days of Korean War. He holds a hat trick for three consecutive, major battles in Korea: Pusan, the Inchon landings, and Chosin Reservoir. Besides carrying his bulky Speed Graphic Camera as a CC photographer, 20-year-old Sgt. Kerr used his M1 admirably. Here is an excerpt from the first of his three campaigns, published in *Leatherneck* magazine in August, 1990:

The Pusan Perimeter, by Frank Kerr

North Korean machine guns and automatic rifles drove us to cover. We winced under our baptism of close-range fire and gasped in the sweltering heat. It was August 7, 1950, and we were spearheading the first offensive of the Korean War. But we surely weren't budging at the moment. So I took a picture. It was lousy.

Marines encountered their first hostile fire into the Naktong rim of the Perimeter. But the column kept advancing—with those Marines leading the way now hugging close to the clanking treads of their beautiful, big, stinking, steel buddies, the tanks. September 1950. (Photography Collection, Harry Ransom-Humanities Research Center, The University of Texas at Austin)

A U.S. jet flies over farmers just five days after North Korea attacked Seoul, marking the beginning of the Korean War. These same jets gave the ground pounders much needed support by slowing down enemy movements. (Photography Collection, Harry Ransom-Humanities Research Center, The University of Texas at Austin)

Enemy artillery had welcomed us earlier, near the village of Ching-dong-ni in extreme southern Korea, and now they were personalizing the reception. Through their sights, we probably looked like easy targets in a shooting gallery, theirs for the potshots. Dead wrong. We were just sweat-drenched moments away from gaining our sea legs as combat Marines.

Second Lieutenant Edward T. Emmelman was some-ticked at us. Or so it seemed, as he sauntered contemptuously above our heads, disdainful of the hell-fire raging around him, suggesting that we take up some other line of work since we seemed to lack the guts for his proud profession. A "mustang" World War II vet, he now led 3rd Platoon, "Dog" Company, Fifth Marine Regiment, First Provisional Marine Brigade.

And lead he did! In minutes he shamed, prodded and inspired us toward our first objective, designated Hill 342—and thus began our epochal march to such blood-hallowed places as the Naktong, Inchon and Chosin and into the illustrious history and heritage of the Corps.

He was gravely wounded the next day, leading as always. But to this moment, 40 years later, I can still see him standing so defiantly as bullets snarled past him like angry hornets and churned dust storms at his boots. Truly a hero to me, then and now, he was a profound influence on all of us. He taught us the meaning of the word Marine, instilled confidence in our leadership and mentally toughened us for the ordeals ahead—from the suffocating summer heat of that day, to the unimaginable winter cold of Chosin, yet to come.

Like all newcomers to combat, I had a lot to learn on both jobs, cameraman and rifleman. During those desperate early weeks, the Brigade—supported by incomparable Marine air—acted as a fire brigade, racing from hot spot to hot spot in the Perimeter to blunt, bloody and counter the North Koreans. The thin ranks of aggressive Marines soon proved that the war was far from lost. Their dash and daring raised morale throughout the beleaguered country, inspired confidence back in the States and sent shocking waves of fear into the enemy. Enemy prisoners spat contempt of everyone else they faced, then confided that they and their comrades were terrified of the "yellow legs," referring to the Marines' canvas leggings.

Suddenly, the Brigade was pulled out of combat and ordered back to Pusan to board ships. We would soon rejoin our parent First Marine Division for the Inchon landing, General Douglas MacArthur's masterful surprise far behind enemy lines.

HEROES

"Me? I'm just a sky jockey flying above, supporting them with my rockets, bombs and a little napalm. But the ground pounders—they're the heroes."

–Capt Ted Williams

No one admired the ground pounders more than the Marine aviators. They worked as a team during their air-ground missions. The jet pilots, with the 1st Marine Air Wing, knew firsthand what the Marine linemen faced. (See chapter entitled *"Hurry! Send Air Support!"*)

Ted Williams, who was flying Panther jets with the VMF-311 Squadron, also saluted the Marine riflemen. Here is what he told me about them:

> The Korean War is fought with infantrymen. With their M1 rifles, automatic rifle power and hand grenades. The Marines up on line—they're the heroes. Me? I'm just flying above 'em, helping support them with my machine guns, rockets, bombs and a little napalm when it's needed. The ground pounders are winning the war.

"He's not heavy. He's my brother." Marines instinctively lend a helping hand to those who fall. Cpl. Little, awarded two Purple Hearts, praised those who aided him. (Sketch by Sgt. John Chalk, Leatherneck *magazine)*

15

SAVING CORPORAL LITTLE

It was a bitter-cold jeep ride from the PIO Radio Section at headquarters to the Seventh Regiment, but cold is what you expect in Korea. I had a lead on a story about a young New Jersey Marine who was a sole surviving son and who had served on the front lines for 10 months. He had also earned two Purple Hearts. Most unusual. *That* is a story!

I met this remarkable Marine's platoon leader, who gave me the story lead, in the First Battalion reserve rest tent. This shelter was huge. I guessed it would hold a whole platoon of 40 men, but it was empty now, probably by design so we could talk freely. Two Yukon oil stoves roared. He lead me to a table close to the stove. Nice spot for the men back in reserve to warm up, regroup, relax and play some cards. The young 2nd lieutenant filled me in on Cpl. Lester Little's family history. Lester's dad, also a Marine, was killed on Iwo Jima. His two brothers, who fought in the Army, died in Europe in WWII. Soon after the Korean War started, Little arrived on a Marine recruiter's doorstep. Like his dad and brothers, he felt it was his turn to serve.

The platoon leader praised Cpl. Little. "He's an unselfish young man. He refused any special treatment. He wanted to serve with his fellow Marines—on the front lines of Korea. Would the rest of us make such a gallant gesture?"

A few minutes later, Cpl. Little entered. During our get-acquainted session, before the taping started, I learned more about him. He was not afraid to smile, and he made friends easily. He was a tough New Jersey kid. His hometown was Phillipsburg. He was only 20, and was a Marine's Marine. He was close to six feet tall and weighed about 190 pounds. He was a perfect BAR man.

Cpl. Little could have served stateside. But he refused to take advantage of the "sole surviving son" rule, which he thought silly.

Contrary to popular belief, "only sons," "the last son to carry the family name," and "sole surviving sons," must register with Selective Service and can be drafted. When a family member has been lost as a result of military service, the remaining family members must be protected insofar as possible. The original "protection" law was passed in 1948, after WWII. Yet Lester Little refused to be exempt from combat. He told me that did not want to hide behind any "silly rule." He wanted to do his part in the Korean War.

The protection rule came to be because of the fate of the five Sullivan Brothers in WWII. All five Sullivans joined the Navy soon after Pearl Harbor and asked to serve on the same ship. They were assigned to the USS *Juneau*, a light cruiser. In a naval battle off Guadalcanal, it was torpedoed and sunk by a Japanese submarine on November 13, 1942. All five brothers died. Their story came to national attention through headlines and a movie, *The Fighting Sullivans*. The film immortalized the five brothers from America's heartland, Waterloo, Iowa. Since then, the military discourages family members from serving in the same unit. Similarly, I know married friends who will not fly together on the same plane for fear of leaving their children without parents.

I was honored to interview Corporal Little. He asked that we play down the sole survivor aspect of the story. "And for God's sake, don't use the word 'hero,' 'cuz I ain't," Little said. This was the first time the subject of an interview tried to spell out the rules to his interviewer. I could see his side. So I thought about it and told him I had an idea how to do the story. I led off with a few words about Christmas and about the New Year in Korea, and about what the holidays meant for some of the troops going home. Then I brought him in. This story was too good to ignore his family's military history. I knew once the tape was rolling, Cpl. Little would go along with the questions, and he did. Here is the transcript from the broadcast on the *Marine Corps Show* from Hollywood, California, in January 1953:

INSTANT HERO

Cpl. Lester Little, a sole surving son winning two Purple Hearts, became a new Marine hero after the public heard his story broadcast from Korea.

HILL: From the First Marine division in Korea, this is Marine Radio Correspondent Dick Hill. This week the men finished opening their Christmas packages and, like the folks back home, had a final taste of the turkey that was left from the holiday meals. Behind them now are the memories of 1952. For the people back in the states it was memories like the Brooklyn Dodgers giving the New York Yankees a run for their money. Watching Marilyn Monroe grow in popularity every day. And of course, the Presidential election. But for the Marines in Korea, it was memories like Bunker Hill. Sniper Ridge. The Hook. And something the whole world waited for, the visit of Dwight D. Eisenhower, the President-elect. The arrival of 1953 to some people means just another year. But to one Marine in particular, Lester E. Little, of Phillipsburg, New Jersey, holder of two Purple Hearts, it means that he'll be leaving Korea. Lester, how long have you been here in Korea?

LITTLE: I've been here in Korea twelve months.

HILL: And how long during that time were you up on line?

LITTLE: Ten and a half months I was up on line.

HILL: Lester, what operations did you participate in over here?

LITTLE: I was up on Outpost Two, 190, and Bunker Hill.

HILL: And to the Marines over here, those are familiar hot spots in Korea.

LITTLE: Yes they are.

HILL: Corporal Little, what were your duties on all those outposts?

LITTLE: I was an automatic BAR man.

HILL: That's the BAR? The Browning Automatic Rifle?

LITTLE: Yeah! The BAR is the firepower of the fire team.

HILL: Well, Lester, you are the holder of two Purple Hearts. What outposts were you wounded on?

LITTLE: I was hit up on Outpost Two and up on 190.

HILL: And what was going on at the time? Mortar fire? Is that how you got wounded?

LITTLE: Yeah! I was standing in the trench and I heard the mortar leave the tube. But it was too late. It got me.

HILL: Well, Corporal Lester Little, how does it feel to be getting away from Korea and have a chance to start next year—1953—without having to worry about being up on the front lines? Around all that enemy fire power?

LITTLE: It's pretty hard to express my feelings, but I'll be glad to get away from it all. I sure won't miss that mortar fire up on line.

HILL: Well, I might explain to the folks back home that you do look like a happy Marine. All smiles. And with all you've been through, I'm sure that the memories of this past year—1952—will probably stay with you for quite awhile. Corporal Little...I understand that you come from quite a military family.

LITTLE: Yes I do. My Father was a Marine in the last war. World War II. He was killed on Iwo Jima. And I had two brothers who were killed in Germany.

HILL: And you're the last son? (Pause.) That must mean you're a sole surviving son, then.

LITTLE: That's right. I am.

Marine helicopters saved hundreds of lives by air lifting wounded—including Cpl. Little—to nearby MASH (Mobile Army Surgical Hospital) centers. (Author's Collection)

COLD LESSON

During one of our swimming classes in boot camp, some of the guys were goofing off. Our DI made us stand at attention for five minutes on the edge of the pool in our wet bathing suits. That wouldn't be so bad, but it was December and the temperature felt close to freezing.

HILL: Was it necessary for you to come over here to Korea?

LITTLE: No. It was not necessary for me to come to Korea.

HILL: Did you request combat duty? Or, what's the story?

LITTLE: I requested combat duty. I wanted to come over here and do my share with the other boys.

HILL: Well, it certainly looks like you're doing more than your share over here in Korea, Lester. By the way, how old are you?

LITTLE: I'm 20. Twenty years old.

HILL: Well, Lester Little, you've been in Korea long enough to know how the folks back home can help the men who will be over in 1953. Would you please tell the home front what they can do?

LITTLE: Be happy to. The folks back home can donate blood to their blood bank as often they can. And mail. They can write letters as often as they can to the boys over here. And something else. They can say a few prayers for us over here once in awhile.

HILL: Well, you heard it, folks. From someone who knows. Please give some blood. Write some letters. And say some prayers. That's how you can support the troops here in Korea. It was a pleasure to speak with you, Corporal Lester E. Little. And I know that all the folks back home, not only in Phillipsburg, New Jersey, but all over the country, are proud of you, and proud of all the other men, now serving in Korea. This is Marine Radio Correspondent Dick Hill returning you to the *Marine Corps Show* in Hollywood, California.

We heard feedback that the broadcast was well received by the listeners. Some letters came in saying how happy they were that Cpl. Little was leaving Korea. Others did not think he should have been there in the first place. Of course, as the corporal mentioned, he volunteered for combat duty in Korea.

When Steven Spielberg's movie *Saving Private Ryan*, starring Tom Hanks, came out, I immediately thought about Corporal Little. Someone up there watched over him and saved him from the enemy mortar fire and sniper fire. His story should be in the *Guinness Book of Records*. It was a first in the Marines—in all the military, for that matter—for a surviving son to be in combat in Korea for ten months and to win two Purple Hearts. That is the tale of a hero.

Marine F9 Panther jets being loaded with bombs at the VMF-311 Squadron, 1st Marine Air Wing, Pusan Korea, June 15, 1953. Ted Williams flew out of this base. (Marine Corps Photo/Sgt. Giese)

16

"HURRY! SEND AIR SUPPORT!"

Teamwork is an important part of war. No one did it better than the Marine Air-Ground Team that I saw in action and reported on in August of 1952. Three sleek, black F9 Panther jets delivered a scorching knock-out punch to the charging Chinese soldiers on the Hook. It was a key ridge on the MLR that the Marines were trying desperately to hold. Ownership of it went back and forth between the Marines and the enemy. It was ours again. It took napalm bombs to force the Chinese back to their own line. The air-ground performance was an experience I will never forget.

MSgt. Joe Hensley and I were there for the possible air strike story that would be broadcast on the *Marine Corps Show*. We had tried to record one earlier but it never came off. This one looked like a "go" because the enemy was already getting ready to do something big. Joe was operating the tape recorder, and I did the play-by-play. For power we used a small Briggs and Stratton generator. We set it up some 100 feet behind us to hide any sound that could leak into our microphone. It could get pretty noisy, but so would the jets and bombs if the air strike took place.

We were located on the side of a hill where a deep trench hid us from any possible sniper fire. (Their snipers were expert riflemen. And experienced in patience, too. They would wait hours just to squeeze off a good shot.) Joe, who held rank and years on me, watched over me like a son. He reminded me to keep my head down as much as possible. But I would have to look over the ridge to report the action. We wore a flak jacket (an armored vest), helmet, and green fatigues tucked into our field boots. As all Marines do, we carried weapons. I had my M1; Joe had a carbine and a .45 strapped to his web belt. We were ready to go to work, two radio correspondents hoping to score a big story for the public.

After the air support story was broadcast, I was asked if I was scared taping it being so close to all our friendly fire. "No," was my answer. "Our Marine flyers know their pin-point bombing drill quite well."

As I discovered, the air-to-ground communications had to be on the money. A little off, or a little late, could mean missed opportunities or deaths from friendly fire. The jets, flying up to 200-miles-an-hour for this kind of an air strike, did not have much room for error. The air support was coming from the VMF-311 Squadron, 1st Marine Air Wing, headquartered in Pusan, Korea. The ground team was the 1st Platoon of "Able" Company, 1st Battalion in the 7th Regiment. Representing them was a pilot who was the observer. He and a Marine radio operator were about 20 yards to the right of us. They were also hunkered down in a trench. Their job was give an accurate overview of the battle field. They had to let the pilots know where the opportunities were to strafe and bomb without getting too close to the Marines protecting their position on the Hook. The pilot, as observer, knew the capabilities of the aircraft, and he attended the briefings of the ground troops so he knew their plans. He was the key to success in this operation.

Here is the broadcast from August 1952 that was heard nationally on the *Marine Corps Show:*

———————————

HILL: From the First Marine Division in Korea, this is Radio Correspondent Dick Hill. We're broadcasting from a front line position called the Hook, a hotspot for the 7th Marine Regiment. The men in the First platoon, "Able" Company, are responsible for holding the hill. At all costs. And that's not as easy as it sounds. We're facing the Communist Chinese line, where we can see some activity on their side. And close to me is Master Sergeant Joseph Hensley, the NCO in charge of radio correspondents, who's operating our recording equipment. And a dozen or so yards from him is a Marine 1st lieutenant jet pilot who's acting as an observer today. If the enemy activity warrants it, he'll be calling in an air strike. And with the observer is an alert radio operator—a Marine corporal. It's a team that has worked together in the past. Any jet planes that may be used today will be coming from the far southeast corner of Korea. That's Pusan, where the famous VMF-311 Marine squadron is based. Chances are it'll be the F9 or F4 Panther jets that we'll see. Oh, oh, I see something. With my field binoculars I'll be able to put a finger on what's out there. Oh my God! Here they come. It's what they predicted for today. The Communist Chinese—the gooks, as the Marines call them, are leaving their lines—in masses. I'd estimate a hundred—or more. They're too far away for their burp guns to be effective. (Pause.) I just heard our observer. He gave some instructions in code. I'm sure it was something like: "Hurry! Send in air support! The Marines need help." The air support can't come any too soon, for my money. The Chinese are still out of range for our Marines, but they'll let go first with .30 mm machine guns. Then the Browning Automatic Rifles—I'd hate to be in front of one of those babies— then the blitz of M1 rifles for more fire power. But the real fireworks will come from the Panther jets with their napalm bombs. The Marines on the front lines have utmost respect for the First Marine Air Wing. And vice versa. I've heard the pilots praise the men— ground pounders—they call them. And the Marines call the pilots sky jockeys. But there's a genuine admiration between the two units—both fighting the Korean War and both skilled at what they do. (Pause.) I hear jets. I see one. Now two. They're coming in. And they'll be coming in fast—around 200 to 250 miles an hour. It's the observer's job—not too far away from us—to help the pilots do some pin-point bombing.

The author by a jeep in the 7th Regiment. It was the motor pool's workhorse, racking up more miles in the war than any other vehicle. (Author's Collection)

RIGHT ON

The jets' pin-point bomb-ing saved the day for Ma-rines on the Hook. (See facing photo.)

He'll supply the coordinates to put the jets on track. And these pilots are good. They did most of their battle training at Cherry Point, North Carolina, long before they arrived in Korea. I see three jets—and it's obvious they see the Chinese because they're starting to buzz them. And no practice runs for these guys. When they come in, they come in firing with their .50 caliber machine guns. And here comes a bomb. Right in the middle of the enemy. (SOUND: Bomb explosion.) I'd call that a direct hit. You must have heard it. What a sight. The napalm routed the enemy—they're running every which way. Like a Chinese fire drill, as our guys call it. Some of their men are on fire. Good God, that napalm is deadly. Here comes another jet—and still more heat for the enemy. (SOUND: Exploding napalm bomb.) I'd hate to be them. The napalm is scorching the charging Chinese. And scorching the ground and everything around it. It's a chemical substance—napalm is a substance that thickens gasoline. The thickened, or jellied, gasoline is used for making incendiary bombs—what the Marine jet pilots are using today. Also used in flame throwers. Here comes another run by the Marine jets. (SOUND: Bomb explosion.) Oh, here's something. What our riflemen have been waiting for. I mean here's our chance to target practice. They're opening fire on the confused Chinese. Some even moving toward our lines—to get away from the napalm. Oh, the god-awful smell of napalm. (BACKGROUND SOUND: Machine gun & rifle fire.) Oh, oh! They're like sitting ducks. We've got 'em where we want 'em. What a massacre. But the enemy deserves what they're getting. With all the sniping and midnight raids on our men. It's well known that the Chinese despise the Marines and go out of their way to target our men. Oh, here's something. One of the Marines is standing on the ridge. Jumping up and down—waving at the jet pilots. He's

Fire and smoke billowing from an enemy target. The author and MSgt. Joe Hensley taped this air strike in August 1952. (Photo Courtesy Joe Hensley)

celebrating. Giving the "thumbs up" signal. Now the planes are moving out. Back to their base at Pusan. I'm sure their battle report will have a great big word of success written on it somewhere. I mean today was our day. I'd estimate 50 or more Chinese casualties. We sure sent them a message. It'll take 'em awhile to regroup. But we don't want to gloat too much. They'll be back. But we'll be ready for them. Great teamwork today from our Air-Ground Team. The Marines in the air and the Marines on the ground. A winning combination. This is Marine Radio Correspondent Dick Hill speaking from the front lines of Korea, returning you to the *Marine Corps Show.*

The home front responded enthusiastically to the air support story. One listener wondered why the United Nations did not use all air power in Korea. Why bother with ground troops, he inquired. The Korean War was a foot soldiers' war. Military leaders called it a stationary war. Thanks to air support, the men on the front lines did get the helping hand they needed, as in the air-ground taped story described. The Marine Panther jets were the ideal ground-support planes to protect the ground troops. They were fast and maneuverable. What a beautiful sight to see when they were in combat. One of the most distinctive sounds in the war was fighter jets. They had a whine or purr that was a sound of beauty. There was no mistaking them when they started their descent into action. In the early days of the Korean War, the Soviet MiG-15's were used. Besides the Soviets, who wore Chinese uniforms, the jets were flown by the Chinese and North Koreans. Our aviators could easily tell who was flying them, as the Soviets were World War II veterans and superior pilots. Their disguise tactic did not work. The Soviets knew all the tricks in the air and gave our B-29 bombers trouble. They pulled back their air support in the latter part of the war. From 1952 on, the United Nations led in air power.

Some trivia. One of the words in the transcript from the broadcast is "gloat." It is outdated. Today the word used is "tout." We hear it all the time during NFL football games. It is used when a player demonstrates in a bush-league manner, or gives an overt gesture. Sometimes they get fined for "touting." Marines don't "tout" (or gloat) much. But if they do it's for a good cause. The young Marine who was celebrating, of sorts, on top of the Hook ridge after the victorious air strike, could not hold it back. He was demonstrating for all the men in his rifle platoon. They had many touch-and-go days holding the enemy in check. Occasionally they were toe-to-toe in battle. On that day, in August 1952, with the support of the First Marine Air Wing, they had the extra weapons they needed to stop the enemy cold. If that rifleman had not done the celebrating, I am sure I would have. It was that kind of occasion.

Capt. Ted Williams ready for another bombing mission. The Marines on the MLR appreciated the air support from the 1st Marine Air Wing. (Marine Corps Photo)

Marilyn Monroe with Marine Col. William Jones on February 16, 1954, after her stand-ing-room-only USO performance in Korea. Jones commanded the 1st Marine Regiment. (AP Photo)

17

"MARILYN IS COMING..."

There were more than bullets flying around Korea. Rumors, too. During my tour in 1952–1953, they were running rampant. Some of the scuttlebutt that I recall: *"Start packing. Truce signing tomorrow." "John Wayne movie tonight." "The Russians will enter the war." "Battle pay to double." "Two replacement ships are coming."* And the best one of all, *"Marilyn Monroe is coming to see us."* Most of the time the rumors never materialized. Case in point: *"Battle pay to double."* It stayed right where it was at $45.00 a month. Sadly, some of the men had counted on the rumor—and the extra money—and bet it away in poker games.

Scuttlebutt is as old as the wind and the sea. Matter of fact, it started on ships. "Scuttlebutt" was a keg of water on board ship which sailors would gather around and swap tales and gossip. In Korea, the rumor mill covered a hodgepodge of subjects. The progress of the war, for example, was always discussed. Rumor had it that we better be packing for home. The war would be over by October 1952. Yet the peace negotiations dragged on at Panmunjom for nearly another year. It had happened before, too. The Marines that landed on Inchon got the word they would be home by Christmas 1950. But it never happened. Many of those Marines were later in the bloody Chosin Reservoir battle and never did get home.

I never paid much attention to the grapevine. That is because I got burned by a rumor when I was about eight years old. I loved the double features that played on Saturdays in Minneapolis. But money was tight so I could not always go. My older brother, Kenny, came running up to the house with a couple of his buddies. Out of breath, he told me he had some scuttlebutt about our Uncle Bill Severts. He was our only relative with any money. He drove a big black Packard and was going to pick us all up and take us to a Roy Rogers and Trigger movie. Boy, was I excited.

SCUTTLEBUTT

We all get suckered in with false promises. Usually they're too good to be true.

Kenny told me to wait on the front step and watch for the car. Well, I did. I waited, waited, and waited. No Packard. No Uncle Bill. No brother Kenny, either. Like older brothers did in those days, he ditched me. He took off with his pals to the Rialto Theater. Boy, was I ever suckered. I never did get to see that Roy Rogers and Trigger film.

A few of the guys were gossip junkies. And some liked to start their own rumors (much like my brother). I was at the supply tent trading in my ripped armored vest for a new one when the supply clerk, a husky corporal, asked if I had heard the news.

"What news?" I innocently asked.

"Haven't you heard?" he nearly shouted.

Whenever you hear "Haven't you heard?" you immediately think you are the only one that missed something. At first I did not realize he was pulling my leg, that he was planting a scuttlebutt seed. "Heard what?" I anxiously asked.

"About the big push. They are getting ready to attack. This looks like the big one," he said.

"When's it coming?" I asked, taking the bait, but still not sure if he was kidding or not.

"The next moonless night. It's gonna be one of these mass charges with their bugles and everything. It could be the end for lots of us," he continued.

Finally a light went on. This guy was nuts. I told him he was full of it.

He continued his pitch like a slick aluminum-siding salesman. "Okay, don't believe me. But over in weapons—I wasn't supposed to say anything—but they're getting ready for something big. And in a couple of nights there's no moon. Perfect conditions for something big."

This poor guy did not have enough to do. So he tried to have a little fun between taking inventory and supplying the troops. One of these times the Sgt. Major would overhear him and straighten him out. Maybe he would lose a stripe or two.

On the way back to our PIO Radio tent, I ran into an old buddy, Cpl. Charlie Stevenson. He was a clerk for the colonel in G-1 (Personnel). We came to Korea together on the USNS *Gen. John Pope* ten months before. We were part of the 20th draft. We even got seasick together. I had been sicker than a dog for two days. Then it was over. And no seasickness on the way back. I was cured. Anyway, the first thing Charlie said was: "Have you heard?"

Oh, no, I thought to myself. Not more scuttlebutt. I've had enough for one day. But he was pretty reliable. And being in G-1 he was privy to lots of inside information. "Heard what?" I asked. I could tell he was anxious to share some news with me.

"Marilyn Monroe is coming to Korea," he blurted out. It was like he was withholding the information for weeks—and had to get it out. "She'll be with the USO Camp Show."

"How do you know?" I quizzed Charlie.

Kim, a South Korean orphan boy, was our PIO radio tent houseboy. (Author's Collection)

"Because the special services officer told the colonel," he fired back.

"When?" I asked.

"In about a month."

"How many people know?"

"Not many. Just special services and the colonel."

"And you—and now me," I reminded him.

"Yeah. But that's all."

Marilyn Monroe was about the hottest thing to hit the movies. Marines loved her walk—and her movies. Twentieth Century Fox was betting she would be bigger than Betty Grable. And so far we had only seen her in bit parts. While in Korea, I saw *The Asphalt Jungle* and *All About Eve*. Her signature films, *The Seven Year Itch*, *Bus Stop*, and *Some Like It Hot*, were a few years away.

Originally named Norma Jeane Baker, Marilyn Monroe was quite a piece of work. An orphan with a mentally disturbed mother, she was only 16 when she married her 21-year-old neighbor, James Dougherty. The poor guy never knew what he had until he saw her on the big screen. By then they were divorced. The camera was her first big love. Starting her career as a model, her calendar pose showed the stuff she was made of. Then Hollywood called. They made her a blonde. And shaped her into an international figure. The media invented a new word for her: "Superstar." And Marilyn lived up to the image.

The troops in Korea loved her movies. Now we were going to see her in person. I had already seen a few USO Shows at Division Headquarters. Some of the headliners included Bob Hope, Francis Langford, Mickey Rooney, Danny Kaye, Debbie Reynolds, Groucho Marx, Al Jolson, and Jack Benny. As they did in World War II, the USO Camp Shows performed hundreds of times for battle-weary troops in Korea and for wounded GIs in the evacuation hospitals in Japan. In my book, the USO was the best. The morale and support they provided the armed forces was unbeatable.

The rumor that Marilyn was coming to Korea in 1953 was premature. And yes, lots of troops were disappointed. When she did arrive the following year, many of us were gone. I had completed my Korean tour and was soon discharged from the Marines. Her appearance was a fluke. She had just married the New York Yankee baseball star, Joe DiMaggio. As newlyweds they were on a trip to Japan. Marilyn, against her new husband's wishes, decided to take a side trip to visit the armed forces still serving in Korea. One good thing, the war was over. It made her trip much safer. But can you believe it? Joe DiMaggio let his bride go alone. He stayed in Tokyo. People in the know hinted that this was the beginning of the end for their marriage. Joe resented the fact that Marilyn was more popular than he was. But it was an "apples and oranges" kind of thing. He had his fans; she had hers. The poor guy did not understand that. They divorced a few months later.

SIDE TRIP

Would you do it? Take off in the middle of your honeymoon to put on some USO shows in Korea? Marilyn Monroe did. She was in Japan with her new husband, Joe DiMaggio. She invited him to take the side trip with her, but he declined. She came alone.

Marilyn Monroe packed 'em in. Over 100,000 UN troops enjoyed her USO shows.

Thanks to the GI Bill, I was back in school at the University of Minnesota when I read about Marilyn's "tour of duty" in Korea. The rumor I had heard when I was there was true. Marilyn finally did visit the Marines and other UN forces. It was February 16, 1954 when she appeared with the USO Camp Show "Anything Goes." Greeting her was Col. William K. Jones, Commander of the First Marine Regiment. According to the reviews, it was a sensation. She performed in ten shows over four days. The audiences totaled more than 100,000 of the United Nations' forces. The UN said it was the biggest gathering for any one star in Korea.

One of the lucky fellows in the crowd was 2nd class David Geary, a Navy medic. He brought his new Argus camera to the show. As he hunted for a seat, someone spotted his medic insignia and offered him a choice second-row seat. Throughout the performance he focused his camera at the stage and took lots of shots. You can see his classic photos today—some 50-plus years later—at the Smithsonian Institution.

Let's suppose that Joe DiMaggio had accompanied his wife to Korea, and that he had made a brief stage appearance with her during the USO Camp Show. Can you image the extra impact from this event had Joe tagged along? It would have showcased America's most popular couple in the entertainment and sports world. But close friends said that Joe had both a jealous and selfish streak. He did not want anyone else looking at his beautiful bride. Hollywood was a whole new playing field for Joe DiMaggio. Joe should have stuck to baseball.

Marines and other UN troops enjoyed outdoor movies and USO shows in settings like this. (Sketch by TSgt. Tom Murray)

A letter from home was a powerful morale builder. (Sketch by John Chalk, Leatherneck *magazine)*

18

MAIL CALL

Happiness for a Marine in Korea was getting a mittful of mail, and you usually did when you moved off the front lines back to Regiment reserve, where mail was held up and waiting. If you were really lucky, a box of cookies would be in your stash.

The connection to home and family is important for morale in the military. Mail was a high priority. It was even logged in each Regiment's monthly command diary that the Commandant and his staff reviewed. There were times when a guy got shut out. It happened to me. But your buddies were quick to include you in their windfall. "Hey, listen to what they're doing back home," they would mention. Or, "Wanna see this picture of my girlfriend in her new bathing suit? But don't drool on it, please."

One mail call that stands out for me was the letter I received from the family of a Marine that I had interviewed. He had made national news and become a hero. His family in Trenton, New Jersey, wrote to say they appreciated the information I had sent filling them in about their son's capture by two Chinese soldiers. Sgt. Francis Grunert, a machine gunner with the Seventh Regiment, had been captured on the Hook, a high ridge on the MLR. His position was overrun by the enemy, and he was pulled away. Luckily, he was saved three hours later. He was tagged "The Lucky Leatherneck."

I still have that letter, thanks to the advice of an old-timer, who said to hold on to it.

It was shortly later when I interviewed another sergeant from New Jersey, Sgt. Richard Albright. As he pointed out, his hometown, Passaic, was several hundred miles northeast of Trenton, on the Passaic River. I had heard about Albright's musical ability and went to the Eleventh Marines to do a story on him. An operations sergeant, he

Many of the Marines I taped were from New Jersey, including Richard Albright, the singing Marine. The Corps sure got their share of men from the Garden State.

had a letter he was sending home in the way of a song. He sang it accompanied by his guitar. I taped it in November 1952. Here's the transcript from the *Marine Corps Show* that aired on NBC Radio from the beautiful Palladium Ballroom in Hollywood, California:

———————————

HILL: From the First Marine Division in Korea, this is Marine Radio Correspondent Dick Hill, inviting you to join the Marines in their bunkers or tents right now. By means of a taped recording, you'll hear a "Message from a Marine." You don't have to travel far in Korea to run into musically-minded Marines. In the various outfits it's possible to hear everything from accordions to mouth organs. And Sgt. Richard Albright, serving with the Eleventh Marines as an operation sergeant, continues to play his favorite instrument, the guitar, just as he did back in the states. Dick, where 'bouts are you from?

ALBRIGHT: Passaic, New Jersey.

HILL: And where did you get the guitar?

ALRIGHT: This belongs to Special Services.

HILL: Dick, did you ever play your guitar other than for amusement back home?

ALBRIGHT: No. It was strictly amusement.

HILL: What about over here? Do you entertain the troops quite a bit?

ALBRIGHT: Well, we get together now and then. And we have a songfest, if that's what you call entertainment.

HILL: Well, I bet it gives the men a chance to relax. And gives them a little fun singing some of their favorite tunes.

ALBRIGHT: (Plucking guitar.) Yes. And we get a few laughs out of it, too.

HILL: Dick Albright, how long have you been in the Marine Corps?

ALBRIGHT: A little better than six years.

HILL: And during those six years, how long have you played a guitar?

ALBRIGHT: Approximately three years.

HILL: Well, that's a pretty productive way to spend your free time, isn't it?

ALBRIGHT: Yes it is. I've had a lot of good times with this guitar.

HILL: Well, Dick, getting to our big question. What message would you like to send back home for your "Message from a Marine?"

ALBRIGHT: (Continuing to play guitar.) Well, I think I should like to send a message to the moms back in the states. See, this isn't just for the moms with the Marines, but it is dedicated to all the mothers who have servicemen in Korea. This is for all the military. For the Army, Navy, and the Marines. (Leads into song, singing.)

Dear Mom. The weather today was cloudy and damp.

Your package arrived, but was missing a stamp.

Your cake made a hit with all the boys in the camp.

How they loved it...and Mom, the food is okay.

Don't worry your head, I sleep pretty well, but miss my old bed.

And oh, how I wished they'd make this Army coed.

Still I love it...

One Marine sent home a special message for all the mothers with servicemen in Korea.

If you should run into a certain you-know-who

Please do this for me. Give her a kiss for me

And tell her to write me nightly.

Dear Mom. The bugle just blew.

That's all for tonight. Tomorrow's a big day with plenty to do.

I like it here, but I'm lonesome for you.

Still I love it, Dear Mom.

HILL: (Over guitar music.) For all the moms who have servicemen in Korea, that was Sgt. Richard Albright of Passaic, New Jersey, adding music to his letter back home. This is Marine Radio Correspondent Dick Hill from the First Marine Division in Korea hoping you'll join us again for another "Message from A Marine." We return you now to the *Marine Corps Show* in Hollywood, California.

(Guitar music up full a few seconds, then fades out.)

———————————

The above is a transcript from the taped recording with Richard Albright, who sang his rendition of the popular song *Dear Mom*. Who could imagine that a tough Marine like Dick Albright could send home such a sentimental letter? I can still picture him in his tent singing and strumming on his guitar. The broadcast touched a lot of listeners. The singing Marine received fan mail for weeks. His platoon buddies called him the "new Perry Como."

28 December 1952

Cpl Richard Hill

Dear Corporal,

A few lines to let you know that Mrs Grunert and I received your letter answering our request for a copy of Francis Grunert's interview with you and we certainly appreciate your taking time to write us about the same and informing us how to go about trying to get a copy of Recording.

We have started to try to find out about same and will be very glad to let you know if we are successful or not. Meantime let me again express our thanks to you and also your kind thoughts for a happy 25 December to us and all people back here at home we hope that you and all Marines and service people home and abroad had a very merry Xmas and Happy New Year. Thanking you again

Sincerely yours
Mr & Mrs F. P. Grunert
6 Warner Drive Trenton (9) N.J. U.S.A.

A "Thank You" from the Francis Grunert family, December 29, 1952. (Author's Collection)

FIRST MARINE DIVISION

CHAPEL

WELCOME

Picture of the 1st Marine Div. Chapel on this souvenir brochure. Serving all religions, it was a popular hangout for Marines. (Author's Collection)

19

GOD IN KOREA

"Going to church, huh, Hill? What's the hurry? It's not even Sunday."

Always the joker, MSgt. H.B. Wells, was referring to my next assignment, to interview a Navy Chaplain. Wells assumed I was doing the taping at the First Marine Division Chapel, just a few hundred yards away from our PIO radio tent. However, Joe Hensley and I figured the radio broadcast would have more impact if we recorded the story at battalion level, close to the front lines. Chaplain James C. Moore would soon hold a service in a frontline bunker. He agreed to have his sermon recorded.

When coordinating the details with Moore, I learned he was from my home town, Minneapolis. He was a tall Swede with light brown hair and a big smile. I spent maybe 30 minutes with him to get some background for the story. He was most congenial and gave me all the information I needed.

He explained that the tradition of chaplains in battle went back to the Middle Ages. Their presence was a good morale builder for the men who attended their services or sought their advice. A chaplain can be a minister, rabbi, or priest attached to a unit in the armed forces. Members of the Navy Chaplain Corps are officers and are the spiritual and emotional guides for sailors, Marines, coastguardsmen, and their families.

I asked him why he didn't hold all his services at the division level, where it was a little safer.

"That would be nice, Corporal," he responded. "But I wouldn't be reaching all the men. Part of my flock is in the battle zone. And we're going there tonight."

He added, "The men need to be reminded that God is here in Korea." Chaplain Moore was an all-right guy.

Chaplain Moore thought his congregation could handle a familar and nearby subject – death.

Here is a transcript from the *Marine Corps Show* broadcast in July 1952. The taping took place just off the MLR, close to the First Battalion, Seventh Regiment:

CHAPLAIN: Our Father who art in heaven, hallowed be Thy name. Thy kingdom come, Thy will be done on earth as it is in heaven.

HILL: (Over chaplain in background.) From the fighting front of the First Marine Division in Korea, this is Marine Correspondent Dick Hill. The Lord's Prayer is not saved just for Sundays in Korea. Regardless of the day, Marines of all creeds and religions up and down the front lines join Navy Chaplains in worship, despite the hazardous surroundings. A typical day in the life of a chaplain in Korea is no picnic. To hold services for the front line Marines, he and his assistant risk the chance of being shelled by enemy artillery and shot at by Red Chinese snipers. Our Marine Corps microphone has journeyed with Protestant Chaplain James C. Moore, of Minneapolis, Minnesota, in order to bring you this tape recording from Korea. At the present time, our portable tape recorder is located at one of the frontline infantry outfits. You're invited to join these men who have taken time out from their frontline duties to hear the word of God.

CHAPLAIN: (Up full, continuing.) ... yet there was one man who conquered the suffering he had to do in life. His name was Matheson and he was a songwriter. A hymn writer. And he wrote, even though he was blind, this piece: "All light that follows us to all my way, I yield my flickering torch to thee. That in thy sunshine's blaze its day might brighter and fairer be. " There is no need to fear life if you have given yourself to Jesus Christ. One of the greatest fears in our world today is the fear that we will be plunged into a third World War. And there are men who devise all sorts of schemes to keep us from a third World War. And yet, too often, their schemes are no good because their schemes stem from their own fear. It is only when people have founded their faith in God and turn once again to Him and have a faith that is solid without fear that we can hope to have a world that is at peace. And that foundation must begin in your own life and you must begin to build that foundation there by giving yourself to God. We also fear our sins. The sins that wreck our lives. The burden of guilt that we carry around from our sins, fearful that they might be found out. And yet, forgiveness of sins is offered to us through Jesus Christ. A forgiveness of sins that is offered to us through Jesus Christ. A forgiveness that comes when we give ourselves to him. We also fear death. Death is the thing that all of us fear too much because we don't know what death is. We've never been able to look ahead and see just what death means. We just know that life is gone.

HILL: (Over chaplain's sermon.) From a frontline bunker in Korea you have been listening to a portion of Chaplain Moore's sermon. This is just one of his many scheduled services that he conducts seven days a week. From here he will travel by jeep to another frontline infantry company and be ready to start services approximately two hours from now. Chaplain Moore, as well as the many other Navy Chaplains in Korea, does not limit his work to worship services with the men. He is available 24 hours a day to talk and offer advice with men who may have personal problems here in Korea or back in the states. He also is present at medical aid stations where the wounded

COMBAT RELIGION

Men in Korea took advantage of church services as often as they could. They respected the Navy Chaplains that held sermons on the front lines.

return after combat. His tent always has extra magazines and books for men who wish to read. He writes any number of letters to parents and wives of Marines in Korea. You will also find him side by side with men, joking, laughing and offering encouragement. Maybe your son or husband, while this tape recording is in progress, is in his congregation. Chaplain Moore continues his services as the Marines, armed with their M1 rifles, helmets and armored vests, participate in the religious meeting. This is Marine Radio Correspondent Dick Hill speaking from the fighting front in Korea, saying that church doesn't have to be held just on Sundays. As long as there are Chaplains willing to spread the word of God, it can be held anytime, any place. Even on the front lines in Korea. We return you to the *Marine Corps Show* in Hollywood, California.

(Chaplain continues sermon, then fades out.)

————————————

Some listeners were unaware that chaplains served in a war zone. They were surprised that the ministers, priests, or rabbis would risk their lives by putting themselves in such danger. One woman, a Methodist, criticized Chaplain Moore's message about death. She thought that the frontline troops should hear a more encouraging topic, but Chaplain Moore had a handle on the situation. His no-punches-pulled homily about death did not disturb the Marines. Death was a familiar and nearby subject. The chaplain felt it needed some discussion.

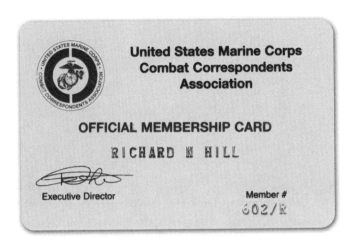

United States Marine Corps
Combat Correspondents
Association

OFFICIAL MEMBERSHIP CARD

RICHARD N HILL

Executive Director

Member #
602/R

The author's membership card. (Author's Collection)

Accepting her fate as an orphan of war, "Miss Hap," a two-week-old kitten, chows down on canned milk piped to her by medicine dropper with the help of Marine Sgt. Frank Praytor. He adopted the kitten after its mother was killed by a mortar barrage near Bunker Hill. (Marine Corps Photo/SSgt. Martin J. Riley)

20

RELAX! IT'S ONLY A WAR

Something I enjoyed from my very first day in the Marine Corps was the humor. It helped cut the tension. Take boot camp, where the non-stop schedule can be upsetting. It did not take much to alleviate the pressure. It could be a word, some clowning, or anything, as long as it reduced stress. Once while limping into our barracks after a grueling ten-mile hike, we were exhausted and pissed off at our drill instructor. We were a sad-looking lot, all sitting on the floor by our bunks. (Marines do not sit or lay on their bed in the daytime.) Dave Maupin from Missouri said this about our DI, "The monster must be in the funeral home business on the side. He wants us all dead." His joke was just what we needed to stop feeling sorry for ourselves. Our anger disappeared. We then went on to shoot the breeze about more important things, like babes and baseball.

The public back home responded favorably to stories and photos of Marines in relaxed settings. Sgt. Frank Praytor, a fellow combat correspondent, was the center of attention when he was caught in a picture feeding a two-week-old Korean kitten canned milk with a medicine dropper. Praytor adopted the kitten after its mother was killed by a mortar barrage near Bunker Hill, one of the hot-spots near the MLR. The baby kitten was appropriately named "Miss Hap." The photo of the great big armed Marine and the itty-bitty kitten was published in 1,700 newspapers via AP. It was taken by Marine photographer SSgt. Martin J. Riley. Many of the publishers reserved the front page for the eye-catching image. Praytor mentioned to me that he got about 30 proposal letters from women. And one from a "fella." Praytor was a writer with PIO and later was assigned to *Stars and Stripes*. A former ad agency man, he lives with his wife in Albuquerque, New Mexico.

Marine platoon leaders know the seriousness of war, but there are times they wish their men would lighten up a little. I was with the First Platoon of Able Company, First battalion, Seventh regiment for a recon assignment. You could feel the tension and anxiety. Then, out of the blue, one of the men in the first squad blurted out: *"Relax, guys. It's only a war!"* Bull's-eye! It broke the tension. That is all it took for the team to unwind. Some quietly laughed. Most smiled. They were the right words at the right time. The young sergeant, a squad leader, instinctively knew something needed to be done. The equally-young second lieutenant platoon leader, just out of officer's training school, was in a better mood. His men were ready for anything now.

Waiting for a jeep, the author "takes five" before his next recording assignment. July 1952. (Marine Corps Photo)

Despite the dangerous conditions in Korea—snipers, mortar and artillery fire and land mines—I saw the Marines as upbeat and in good humor. This kept many of them "up." Besides playing tricks on their buddies, or telling the latest jokes, they liked posting homemade signs. During my radio taping I saw some of their work. They were hanging by bunkers, trenches, latrines, on jeeps, trucks, and in tents. The signs were a good sign, according to Navy Chaplain James C. Moore from Minneapolis. "Laughter," he said, "helps lift the heavy load of war." He went on to explain its psychological side. The upshot was this: It was good therapeutic medicine. According to the chaplain, who worked close with the men, a little bit of humor made happy, healthy Marines. The messages were a sign of the times and helped relieve stress and the worries of what was going on around them. And I could not but help smile at them. Like you would today while driving and seeing a vanity license plate that caught your eye.

Here are the best of them that I ran into while interviewing the men in nearly every outfit in the First Marine Division:

- WILL TRADE FIVE C-RATIONS FOR TWO CLEAN PAIR OF SOX
- WIPE YOUR FEET! (SEEN IN FRONT OF A DIRT-FLOOR BUNKER)
- WE'RE WAITING, IKE! (POSTED RIGHT AFTER EISENHOWER WON THE 1952 ELECTION)
- DEAR ABBY: MY GIRL HASN'T WRITTEN FOR THREE MONTHS. DOES THAT MEAN SOMETHING?

We all got a chuckle from this cartoon in Stars and Stripes. *Combat pay was a big plus for Marines. (Author's Collection)*

- DESIRE CAREER CHANGE. WILL TRADE RE-CON DUTY FOR NICE CUSHY DESK JOB BACK AT DIV. HDQ.
- HOME BY XMAS? WHAT AM I DOING HERE?
- NO SOLICITATIONS. (UNLESS YOU'RE A GIRL)
- ARMED FORCES RADIO: PLEASE PLAY MORE ROSEMARY CLOONEY

Here was one sign the men hated to see when they were off the lines and back in reserve:

No Movie Tonite! Sorry!
Film Didn't Arrive.

The outdoor movies and USO shows were always a good way to relax. The men looked forward to them. Special Services did a swell job putting them on.

Marines are lucky. We get to celebrate two birthdays each year. First, our own personal one. Mine is June 19. Then, on November 10, the big one: the Marine Corps birthday. To my knowledge, no other military service puts on such fanfare into their heritage like the Marines. I've checked with both my brothers, Darrell, Navy and U.S. Air Force, and Kenny, U.S. Army. Neither could recall any birthday celebrations in their respective service. Maybe it is our link to our Founding Fathers that gives the Marines a reason to toot our horn. The Continental Congress established the U.S. Marine Corps on November 10, 1775.

You'd think the celebration would be skipped during the Korean War. No way. It was a great morale booster and a good way to help the men forget the war. At least for a little while. Birthday cake has a way of doing that. For the men up on the MLR, the cooks set up hot kitchens as close to the front lines as possible. Food services outdid themselves for the November 10, 1952 feast that I got in on. There was roast turkey, dressing, giblet gravy, mashed and sweet potatoes, cranberry sauce and birthday cake. It was a meal to remember. Marines on every post and in every time zone in the world enjoyed a similar birthday bash.

Sports were another good way to get your mind off the fighting. Back in reserve there was always someone tossing a baseball or football around. And when you could round up a group, there was volleyball, a great game for exercise and getting rid of tensions.

Marines like a good laugh. Here's a cartoon of the author "recording the Korean War" as seen in Leatherneck *magazine. (Cartoon by John Chalk,* Leatherneck *magazine)*

THIS IS MARINE RADIO CORRESPONDENT, DICK HILL, INVITING YOU TO ANOTHER INFORMAL CHAT WITH THE MEN IN KOREA.

The U.S. Marine Corps attracts lots of sports stars, including Ted Williams, Bob Mathias, Roberto Clemente and Gene Tunney.

The Marine Corps has long been associated with sports. Four former Marines—Rod Carew, Roberto Clemente, Tom Seaver, and Ted Williams—all are honored members of baseball's Hall of Fame. It speaks well for a military service as small as the Marines to have such winners in their ranks. Baseball is just the beginning. There are more famous names that excelled in boxing, football, golf, wrestling, and the Olympics. Along with Ted Williams, here are more popular athletes that served in the U.S. Marine Corps. Check to see how many you're familiar with:

MARINE ATHLETES

Paul Arizin* (Basketball)

Carman Basilio* (Boxing)

Hank Bauer (Baseball)

Patty Berg* (Golf)

Bernie Bierman (University of Minnesota Football Coach)

Rod Carew* (Baseball Hall of Fame)

Roberto Clemente* (Baseball Hall of Fame)

Jerry Coleman (Baseball)

Charley Conerly (NFL Football)

Alvin Dark (Baseball)

Art Donovan Jr.* (NFL Football Hall of Fame)

Verne Gagne (Wrestling)

Frank Goettge* (Marine Corps Football)

Elroy "Crazy Legs" Hirsch* (NFL Football)

Gil Hodges (Baseball)

Lloyd "Butch" Keaser* (Wrestling)

Bob Mathias* (Olympics)

Tug McGraw (Baseball)

Billy Mills* (Olympics)

Ernie Nevers (Baseball/NFL Football)

Leo Nomellini (Football)

Ken Norton* (Boxing Champion)

Bum Phillips (NFL Football Coach)

Tom Seaver* (Baseball Hall of Fame)

Leon Spinks (Boxing)

Ernie Stautner (NFL Football Hall of Fame)

Dan Topping (New York Yankees Team Owner)

Lee Trevino* (Golf)

Gene Tunney* (Boxing Champion)

Bill Veeck (Chicago White Sox Team Owner)

Ray Wietecha (NFL Football)

Ted Williams* (Baseball Hall of Fame)

Members of Marine Corps Sport Hall of Fame

In 2001 the Marines established the Marine Corps Hall of Fame to honor former Marines who have excelled both on and off the athletic field. To learn more about the inductees, see the new National Museum of the United States Marine Corps at the Heritage Center, near Quantico, Virginia. It's stunning. There is lots to learn and worth the visit with your family.

The military's guide book for R&R in Kobe, Japan. (Author's Collection)

21

R&R HOLIDAY

I heard rumors that my name was on the next R&R roster. I was excited, because Rest and Recuperation was a big deal. Everyone needed some goof-off time. An R&R holiday meant a week in Kobe, Japan. Mainly, it was a change in scenery. It got you away from the MLR, C-rations, and combat fatigues. It gave you a chance to do some sightseeing and souvenir shopping. You could even make a phone call home. For some guys it meant their first time with girls. And maybe, trouble.

Where do I begin? With that beautiful Russian girl that the Texas Marine wanted to marry and go AWOL for? Or do I start with that scary plane ride into Kobe? (It almost ended our holiday.) I had better start at the beginning.

It was March of 1953 and the rumor was true. MSgt. Joe Hensely, NCO in charge of radio correspondents in PIO, said he had good news for me: I had been selected for R&R. Two other combat correspondents from my unit were also going. They turned out to be pretty good traveling companions: MSgt. Bob Fugate and SSgt. Don Martin, both combat writers. Fugate was a career Marine from California. He had been a POW after his capture on Bataan in World War II. Tanned and stocky, he was tough as nails and could speak Japanese as well as the natives. This sure gave us an advantage when interacting with the people. Martin was from my part of the world, Des Moines, Iowa. We Minnesotans like to kid our Iowa neighbors, but I think they had the last laugh. Many of the Iowa corn and hog farmers were millionaires. And the rest weren't far behind. They owned some of the richest farmland in all of agriculture. Martin's family was still in farming.

Joe Hensley gave me my travel orders and an orientation booklet about Japan and R&R responsibilities. And a fatherly talk: "Stay away from the water—and the

This C-47 Skytrain transport flew the author and others to Kobe, Japan, for their R&R adventure. (Author's Collection)

girls," he advised. "Both may be contaminated." Two days later our R&R adventure started with a short jeep ride to the Seoul airport. From there it was a two-hour flight to Kobe, Japan. We all looked pretty spiffy. We were freshly shaven and in our dress uniforms. All United Nations forces in Japan were authorized to wear a Korean identification shoulder tab, which we had sewn on the night before. This immediately would signal the Military Police (MPs) that we were not AWOL (Absent Without Official Leave).

But what person trying to avoid the military police would wear their uniform? Oh, well, whatever they want. What a sight. It looked like a United Nations meeting at the Kimpo airport, close to Seoul. The UN forces going on R&R included Americans, Australians, Canadians, and Brits. Our UN allies were some tough-looking cookies. All told there were about 30 of us getting ready to board the U.S. Army Air Force transport plane. It turned out to be a C-47 Skytrain transport, equivalent to a commercial DC-3. The passenger seats on each side of the plane's hull reminded me of the bleacher seats at old Nicollet Park, in Minneapolis, where Ted Williams played one year. Sitting across from one another, we all had a good look at each other. Most of us were smiling, smiling because we were leaving the war zone and headed for rest and recreation, as most of us called R&R. Recuperation was for hospital cases, I always thought.

Coming in to Kobe was a nail-biter. It was about 500 miles due east from Seoul and was supposed to take about two hours. But the unexpected happened. We were all set for a landing when suddenly the C-47 swooped upward. We learned later that an aviation refueling truck was on our runway and the pilot had had to pull up as hard as he could to avoid a collision. We heard the prop motors roar as our pilot zoooomed up, up and away. As the plane suddenly surged upward, most of us fell downward. No seatbelts were provided for the passengers. I landed in the lap of one of the Australian Aussies. Most landed on harder places as there was no carpeting on the deck of the plane. After we caught our breath and went back to our seats, we laughed it off. One smiling, red-headed Army corporal hinted that maybe we would all get Purple Hearts for the debacle. It took another 30 minutes to recircle and get clearance to land. Something similar happened to me landing at O'Hare Field in Chicago years later. Flying in jets then, I was in a huge 747 the moment a private plane was crossing the runway. Trained for such problems, the pilot gave her all she had and pulled up and over the taxiing intruder. The next thing we knew we landed in Indianapolis—instead of Chicago. So apparently obstacles are a problem on runways.

Well, we finally landed in Kobe, one of Japan's six largest cities. The various UN forces all went their separate ways. We chatted with some Marines from different outfits and learned some were going to be billeted in the same hotel we were assigned. We made MSgt. Fugate our unofficial tour guide. He not only had the rank, but he knew his way around Japan and could speak the language. He suggested we try out the rickshaws and head for our lodging. "Always secure your room first," he advised.

"Why?" I innocently asked.

NO CIGAR

As harrowing as the plane ride was from Seoul to Kobe, Japan, we didn't get what seemed like a sure Purple Heart. We all landed on the deck when the pilot swooped up and over a vehicle on the runway.

"Before they give the damn room away to someone else," he boomed, sounding a little like the experienced salesman, world traveler and master sergeant he was.

The rickshaw ride was a good way to relax and get acquainted with Kobe. Up and down the sidestreets our puller cleverly weaved around the masses of people. I could see why they made such a big hit with tourists. They were almost as popular as San Francisco's famous cable cars. Japan was slowly going modern, however, and switching to bicycle taxis. Our lodging was better than expected. It was a converted Kobe hotel for the military. The lobby had a Special Services concierge who helped us with check-in and our itinerary. And the army lieutenant concierge also converted our MPC (Military Pay Certificates) into yen. He cautioned us not to convert too much, as once you change MPC into yen, you can not change yen back into MPC. We also learned that yen would not buy anything in U.S. installations such as the PX, snack bars, mess halls, barber shops, or movies. I found out there was a waiting list for the overseas telephone service, so I would try calling home later.

If you are acquainted with a hostel for bikers, then you have a pretty good picture of my room. Very basic, but clean. A single bed, small dresser, closet, and a bare lightbulb on the overhead. No head in my room, but there was one down the passageway, and it would take some getting used to because unlike the latrines in Korea, this "bathroom" had real running water and a shower to boot. What luxury. This was living. I unpacked my travel bag, organized my gear and got out my small travel book on Japan. I was ready to see Kobe. But like old married men, Bob Fugate and Don Martin were not as anxious to "hit the town" as I was. They wanted to unwind in the lounge, first. They would catch up to me later. So, for awhile anyway, we went our own way. Lt. Nolan, the Special Services officer at the hotel, told me where the best shopping was for servicemen. Besides visiting the PX, he suggested I see the open market place where Kobe sells just about everything. That is where I headed. I wanted to send home some fine china dinnerware to my mother in Minneapolis. And maybe some Japanese artwork, if I could find the right pieces.

As I quickly saw, Japan is a land of great natural beauty. Mountains and hills cover most of the country. Most of the people lived in the cities, like Kobe, Tokyo, Osaka, and Yokohama. I was visiting one of the world's oldest cultures—30,000 years. The land was scarce and was highly prized. Even the mountainsides were fashioned into small terraced plots, some hardly the size of my dad's backyard garden. To make their soil fertile and enable it to produce as much as possible, the Japanese regularly fertilized with excrement of animals and humans. That's why I saw a never-ending procession of "honey buckets" all laden with this valuable fertilizer being transported from the cities to the open-country fields. The Japanese people in their colorful kimonos were small, strong and resourceful. Many, even young children, seemed to be carrying something with little effort. Some had backpacks; others used A-frames, like in Korea, to transport their wares. The narrow streets were jammed with people-

A young Japanese girl at the shop where the author purchased Noritake china in Kobe, Japan, March 1953. (Author's Collection)

227

powered vehicles: bicycles, bicycle taxis, and rickshaws. I saw few automobiles or trucks due to World War II and their lack of petroleum products.

OLDER THAN DIRT

Japan has a 30,000-year-old culture and Kobe was a shopping smorgasbord. The hundreds of shops and vendors offered everything imaginable. I still have the fine Japanese prints and china I purchased over 50 years ago.

My trip to the Kobe market place was a shopping smorgasbord. They sold everything imaginable: from fresh fruits and vegetables and live cackling hens to fine souvenirs, including pearls, silverware, wood carving, ivory, kimonos, and the highly recognized wide-sleeve coats known as *haoris*. And did I mention the countless tiny shops that served tea, sake, and snacks? There was entertainment, too. Several puppet plays were in progress. Each of the principal puppets was operated by three manipulators to bring out amazingly life-like movements. It was fascinating to watch. I wandered around and was impressed with the quality of workmanship in the many craft shops. I spotted the Noritake china that would make a good present for my mom. The merchant did not speak very good English and we had a hard time communicating. As best I could, I told him I would be back later, with my negotiator, MSgt. Bob Fugate. Besides speaking their language, Fugate had some extra stripes that might affect the price. On the way out, a young boy grabbed me by my sleeve. He was only nine or ten years old. But he was in business, too. "Hey, Marine! Wanna girl? My sister's a sherry girl. You wanna see her?" he urged. The shop keeper smiled at me and shooed the young entrepreneur off me. The incident was repeated a half dozen more times on my way back to my quarters.

The next morning Bob Fugate and I tried out the hotel's breakfast for R&Rers. It was delicious. Orange

228

juice. Steak and eggs. Toast. Fried potatoes. Pancakes. Strawberries. Fresh cold milk. And oceans of hot coffee. It sure beat the C-rations we got most of the time in Korea. The Army Special Services ran the hotel for the United Nations forces serving in Korea. But not everyone stayed there.

Some of the men preferred to have more private accommodations. Especially when sales-smart street vendors painted a romantic picture of "a suite of rooms and full-time companionship" for the seven day R&R leave. Often two or three of the men would go together and split costs for the cozy arrangement. In some instances they would have a chance to pick their girl. In other cases it was a catch-as-catch-can proposition. For as long as wars have been fought, and with men needed to fill the ranks, there have been brief encounters between the sexes. The Korean War was no exception.

I was glad I had a chance to see Japan in the 1950s. This was "the before" Japan. Before they started their road back to economic recovery. Flat on their back after their defeat in World War II, the Japanese people refused to stay down. Smart and ambitious, and with the help and influence of the United States, they achieved one of the world's strongest economies. And I saw it all start with Sears & Roebuck catalogs. Great copycats, I personally witnessed merchants duplicating Western fashion for their people. Then, little by little, then a lot by a lot, their products and markets expanded. Today their manufactured products range from tiny computer parts and cell phones to televisions, automobiles, and trucks to giant oceangoing ships. Many of

5-STAR CHOW

A big part of R&R was enjoying the delicious food. Besides American dishes, you could order any kind of Oriental meal you wanted. And a bonus—fresh, cold milk.

our U.S. companies—John Deere, for example—had to retreat from pledges of "No Japanese parts in our products." And General Motors, to improve sales, had to get on the Japanese small-car bandwagon. Today, many of our industries have joint ventures with Japan to improve productivity. And to think the Sears catalog played a part in their turnaround. Pretty good copycats. Now, we're starting to copy *their* technology. Like they say, what goes around, comes around.

On the eve of my last night of R&R, a MP came into the lobby of the Special Services Hotel. He picked me out from the other United Nations forces personnel, and motioned for me to join him. Dressed like they tell you in the books, he had shiny boots that you could comb your hair by. From his open collar, I could see his MP scarf on. Strapped to his side was the shiniest .45 I'd ever seen. And in his hand he kept twirling, from habit, I imagine, a billy club.

"We've got a big problem, sergeant. One of your fellow jarheads was going AWOL."

"Who's that?" I asked.

"We've got him outside—with his girl friend. He's a Pfc. From Texas. I have to give him credit. He can sure pick 'em," the army MP sergeant smiled.

"What's the story?" I inquired. "Did he hurt anyone?"

"No, but he was headed for a ton of trouble if we hadn't stopped him. He was in an off-limits area for military. He was going over the hill—with little miss

Snow White. We caught them at the train station. They were going to Tokyo, so he says."

"Can I see him?"

"Sure. I'll bring them in. Is there a private place where we can sort this all out?"

A second MP, this one down a rank, a corporal, brought the runaway couple in through the lobby. All eyes went to her. She was tall for an Asian. Maybe a couple of inches under six feet. She was all woman. She filled out every inch of her bright red china silk dress for menfolk to marvel at. And they did. The guys in the hotel lobby were mentally measuring her melon-size boobs. (No little lemons for big-thinking Texans.) Her long legs would have been envied by any woman. Tex commented later that her legs were like a "ladder to love." Her snow-white skin and flowing black hair was a bonus. The MP was right. Tex sure picked himself a good one.

Talking to them both, I found out that she was a "white Russian," a name given to members and supporters of the counterrevolutionary White armies which fought against the Russian Red Army in 1917. Erika was a mix of Chinese and Russian and came from Manchuria. This young beauty had swept the young Marine off his feet, and messed up his thinking. The good-looking, six-foot-plus Texan was willing to risk the military catching him to disappear among the throngs of people in Tokyo. The army MPs were obligated to arrest him as he was found in an off-limits area with a prostitute. But they were willing to forget the incident if the Marines would get him back to

A REAL CHINA DOLL

Tex, the young Marine on R&R, sure picked a good one. She was a White Russian from Manchuria. Tall and beautiful, he was willing to go AWOL for her.

THE FORGIVING MP

He could have landed in the brig. But a sympathetic Army MP—knowing about these things—let the Marines straighten the love-sick Texan out.

his unit in Korea, where he would be safe from temptations such as Erika and other ladies of the night. I talked privately with the Pfc. and told him he had no options, that the army was doing him a favor by not pressing charges. And, oh, how the MPs would love to catch a Marine who went astray. It would be another notch on their batons. But this MP, for whatever reason, was offering to set Tex free for getting him back to the fighting Seventh regiment in Korea. Perhaps he realized that the young man needed a helping hand. Some guys go funny during R&R. I spelled this out to him. Tex, nodding yes, but not really agreeing with me, agreed to stay at the Special Services hotel and go back to Korea with us the following morning. His R&R romp was over.

I laughed to myself. It was funny. We were both on a souvenir hunt in the Far East. While I was looking for a set of china, the young Texas Marine wanted a real, live china doll. Well, to each his own. The army MP, who dealt with AWOLs on a regular basis, may have summed up their relationship best. He said that their love for each other was mutual. The Texan had the hots for her, and she had the hots for his R&R money. "That's the trouble with you Marines," he said. " You don't follow the K.Y.P I.Y.P. principle."

"What's that?" I asked as I fell into his trap.

"Keep Your Pecker In Your Pants!" he blurted out.

I was up at 0500 for our trip back to Korea. Most of us took breakfast. A few declined as they wanted as much sack time as possible. It was a different mood than a week ago when we had been flying to Japan and anticipating our new adventure. A little like vacationers in Minnesota. It is always a letdown when the holiday is over. You are returning from your cabin back to home and dragging a fishing boat. And dragging in general. Then you look over to the opposite lane and there is a guy in his Ford pickup headed for the lakes. He is all smiles. Oh, how you would like to change places with him. Well, our party was over. None of us were ready to go back. Especially Tex. He was pissed off all the time we shepherded him back to his unit. But that was okay. After all, no one receiving tough love ever understands the need for it. Fugate, Martin, and I made sure the romantic Texan was returned safe and sound to his platoon leader. We heard he was a good Marine, very valuable on recon jobs, one of the toughest assignments in Korea. A month or so later, I learned that Tex had planned a side trip back to Kobe when his tour of duty was up in the fall of 1953. He was going to look up Erika before leaving for the states. I hope they got together and had lots of little china dolls.

Some returning R&R Marines dutifully visited their Catholic Navy Chaplain.

Of all the military chaplains, I noticed that our Catholic padre was the busiest after an R&R episode. The line outside his tent was long. But that did not keep him from accommodating all the returning men who felt a need for a special confession. They were some of the same guys who tried to do too much in their week in Japan. They were twice as tired as before they left. Now, they needed some extra R&R time—just to recuperate. Oh, well, like my dad always said: "New Year's Eve is for amateurs."

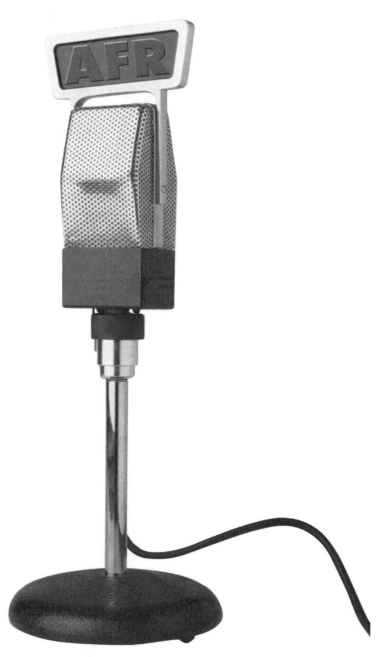

Like a friendly voice from home, Armed Forces Radio was a morale builder for the troops. (Photodisc)

22

GOOD MORNING, KOREA

Thirty-five years before Robin Williams played a disc jockey in *Good Morning, Vietnam*, I was listening to Armed Forces Radio (AFR) in Korea. Our "Good Morning, Korea," also informed, amused, entertained, and pumped us up. For me, the station was an assuring, friendly voice, like listening to a companion from home. Always upbeat, the announcers gave the sports scores (and yes, the Yankees were always winning) and news headlines, and played the music of the day. The radio station was located in Osaka, Japan. Some of the old salts in my tent knew Osaka as a garden spot for some pretty good military duty. Not too far off the peninsula of Korea, Osaka sits by the main island of Honshu at the mouth of the Yodo River on Osaka Bay. The Armed Forces Radio station came in loud and clear for its military audience in Korea and Japan, primarily the enlisted men.

Contrary to the raucous behavior of Williams' character, Adrian Cronauer, the Saigon disc jockey, our AFR announcers did not push the envelope. They were a far cry from Howard Stern's antics on Sirius Satellite Radio. But it is really not a fair comparison, because that was how radio was in the 1950s. They had fun with words, but never went over the top. I enjoyed listening.

I would like to let this chapter serve as a "Thank You" letter to AFR. They fulfilled their mission. Everyone I knew listened. Most tents and bunkers had a radio. (They were not permitted up on line.) Most were Emersons. About half were portable and required batteries, which were hard to get in Korea. Reception wasn't the best in a bunker because of the fickle AM reception. One of our guys, MSgt. H.B. Wells, a combat photographer, had an Emerson shortwave radio. God! What a powerful signal. He could pull in the world, even the enemy. It was fun listening to the many stations from all over the world. Sometimes he would even bring in a ship's broadcast that was in the area. H.B. drew a crowd every time he turned it on.

Similar to my hometown station of WCCO Radio in Minneapolis, Armed Forces Radio in Korea had regular programming throughout the week. Since you grew accustomed to the announcers' voices, they became your friends. The station staff was a mix of the U.S. military services, but mostly from the Army. Andy was one of the Army announcers on the 0600 (6 a.m.) to 1200 (Noon) shift. He never identified his nationality, but he did not have to. He had to be Scandinavian. One of his pet phrases was "Uff da." The words shot out like an arrow toward a target for me. Being from Minnesota you hear the phrase all the time. It is an expression of surprise, astonishment, and sometimes dismay. Andy used it one time in connection with Marilyn Monroe. Still a supporting player, she had made only a few movies with 20th Century Fox. A couple were shown in Korea. One was *All About Eve.* During one of his morning broadcasts he carried on like he was president of her fan club: "She's growing more than just in popularity," he purred. "Have you noticed? She seems to have all the right parts in all the right places. Uff da! She can slip her slippers under my sleeping bag anytime. If my sergeant isn't looking, that is."

You can take the boy out of the country—and send him to Korea—but you cannot take away his love for America's favorite sport—baseball. October was World Series time. I remember the excitement in 1952. It was a subway series between the New York Yankees and the Brooklyn Dodgers. (Not everyone remembers that the Dodgers started out in Brooklyn.) Because of the time difference—Seoul, Korea is 13 hours ahead of New York—the games were delayed and played around noon in Korea. Not many could listen to the whole game, anyway, so it was the highlights everyone wanted to hear. There were some great names in the lineup. For the Yankees: Mickey Mantle, Billy Martin, Phil Rizzuto, and let us not forget the catcher, Yogi Berra. The Dodgers fielded great names, too: Roy Campanella, Pee Wee Reese, Jackie Robinson, and Duke Snider. The New York Yankees won the series in seven games and, even more impressively, won their fourth straight title. No wonder the devil got involved with the musical, *Damn Yankees*, a few years later. Enough is enough, right?

SUBWAY SERIES

In 1952 it was the Brooklyn Dodgers and the New York Yankees. For NY there was Mickey Mantle, Phil Rizzuto and Yogi Berra. The Dodgers had Pee Wee Reese, Roy Campanella and Jackie Robinson. Oh, what a lineup.

Music was a big part of AFR's format. First, there were the Big Band favorites that are still around today: Artie Shaw "Begin the Beguine," Benny Goodman "Let's Dance," Glenn Miller "In the Mood," Les Brown "Sentimental Journey," with Doris Day and Duke Ellington "Take the 'A' Train." Andy and his colleagues also played the hits of the day. They included: "You Belong to Me" with Jo Stafford; "Tell Me Why," The Four Aces; "Wheel of Fortune," Kay Starr; "Rags to Riches," Tony Bennett; and "Doggie in the Window," by Patti Page. Interestingly, many of those songs that hit the charts in the 1950s are still getting air time today. Good music is forever, I guess.

Andy Anderson, our early morning DJ, kept us up-to-date on Hollywood, too. He fed us Hollywood tidbits every day. He was about the biggest movie buff I had ever known. He could even imitate some of the stars, including Jimmy Cagney, Gary Cooper, and someone every imitator does, Edward G. Robinson. With luck, he told us, we would be seeing some of the current flicks out of "flickland," as he liked to call Hollywood. And we did, as the moviemakers wanted to be sure the troops saw the new releases. During my time in Korea I saw *High Noon* with Gary Cooper and Grace Kelly, *The Snows of Kilimanjaro* with Ava Gardner and Gregory Peck, and *Shane* with Allan Ladd, Jean Arthur, Van Heflin, and Brandon De Wilde. I also saw my favorite, *Singing in the Rain*, starring Gene Kelly, Donald O'Connor, and Debbie Reynolds. Each of these movies appears regularly on television, especially on Turner Classic Movies (TCM).

One of the announcers, B.D. Davis, was on nights. A good radio personality, B.D. occasionally read letters from his fans. I remember one in particular:

> Here's one from the Seventh Regiment, a corporal. He's the only one that writes to me with any frequency. Well, anyway. He's mad at me. Says I don't play enough Rosemary Clooney. Well, Corporal. This is your big moment. Because here's one by Rosie. One of her best ...'Tenderly.'

For the next three minutes we enjoyed one of the best hits ever by Miss Clooney. (I used to play it on WBIZ, Eau Claire, Wisconsin, the year before when I was a DJ.)

Armed Forces Radio kept us up-to-date on the heated election between Dwight D. Eisenhower and Adlai Stevenson in 1952. The three major themes put forth were the Korean War, corruption, and a balanced budget. Ike promised to end the war because he knew

THE CLOONEY CLAN

Armed Forces Radio played lots of hits by Rosemary Clooney. This was long before her now-famous nephew, George Clooney, was born and making movies.

firsthand about war. (Most of the military voted for him. We wanted to go home.) Ike also promised to balance the budget. He implied that if housewives could balance the household budget, then so could the government. General Eisenhower won by a wide margin. And the President-elect kept an election promise to visit Korea. Guys on the front lines had signs reading: "We're waiting for you, Ike." Afraid of assassination attempts, his Secret Service people kept his Korean visit under wraps. Very few of us in Korea knew about it. Even our news-hound buddy on Armed Forces Radio, Andy Anderson, was not aware that Ike had arrived in Korea on November 29. While there, Ike made his time productive. Eisenhower helped revive the stalled peace talks and took a side trip to the front lines to mingle with U.S. soldiers. We had heard he wanted to see the Marines, but his trip was cut short due to tight security so he flew back. The public did not know about it until December 6. But the results of his trip are what are important. As a result of his peace-seeking mission, an armistice was signed months later on July 27, 1953. Not all politicians keep their campaign promises, so I send a belated "Thank You" to Dwight D. Eisenhower, who knew his way around the truce table.

The big news in 1953, before I left Korea, was the death of Joseph Stalin in March. At first we thought this event could step up the activity of the Communist Chinese. (They were still getting lots of help from the Soviet Union.) Georgi Malenkov became the Soviet premier. Nothing did materialize. Actually, truce

IN THE NEWS - 1952

Eisenhower wins election

Ike tours Korea battle front

U.S. ends occupation of Japan

negotiations began and eventually the war ended on July 27.

TOP SONGS - 1952

"Tell Me Why"
— *Four Aces*

"Wheel of Fortune"
— *Kay Starr*

"You Belong to Me"
— *Jo Stafford*

In addition to our Armed Forces Radio, we had *Stars and Stripes* for a news source.

It was a pass-along paper, as not everyone had a copy. We always had an issue in our PIO Radio tent at division headquarters. Ted Williams told me in an interview that he read it to keep up on how the American League was doing in 1953. (*S&S* had a great sports section.) I ran into one of its reporters up on the line, as the magazine covered the Korean War like other publications. The reporter told me the roots of *S&S* went back to the Civil War. It really became popular, he said, during World War II when Bill Mauldin, a cartoonist, started his "Up Front," series with the characters Willie and Joe.

Still another good reading source was *Leatherneck*. This award-winning magazine for Marines was a favorite. It also covered the Korean War. I worked closely with two of its artists, Sgt. John Chalk and SSgt. Stan Dunlap. They were both gutsy guys who spent more time on the front lines than they had to. I did not know it at the time, but Chalk drew a cartoon of me broadcasting up on line. It was published in *Leatherneck*, and it caused quite a chuckle from the readers. (Marines love to laugh.)

Like the Egyptian Pyramids, good things last. Armed Forces Radio, *Stars and Stripes* and *Leatherneck* magazine continue to serve the military all around the world. Wherever there are bases, posts, ships, or service members, these three news sources are found,

even some 50 years after they served me and my buddies during the Korean War.

The author, left, in a recording session with Jim Ameche and Major Robert B. Moore at
WGN, Chicago, October 1953. Ameche was host of the Marine Corps Show; *Dick Hill*
the announcer. Moore was CO of PIO, Glenview Naval Air Station, outside of Chicago.
(Marine Corps Photo)

Many Marines sent home this Christmas card that featured a South Korean Papa-San with traditional pipe and dress. (Author's Collection)

23

CHRISTMAS IN KOREA

The subject of Christmas was a sore point for the military in Korea. Not to be confused with Dr. Seuss' mean old Grinch who was trying to *stop* Christmas. The troops were fully for celebrating the greatest holiday of the year, but they had hoped to celebrate it with their families. They were told they would be home for Christmas in 1950. That was General Douglas MacArthur's promise. However, the UN Commander and his military advisors in Tokyo overlooked one little thing: the nearly one million Communist Chinese troops that would be crossing the Manchurian border and entering the Korean War in late 1950. The dynamics of the war changed. So, licking our wounds, the troops spent Christmas in Korea in 1950, 1951, and 1952. Sadly, many never made it home as the war accelerated.

My Christmas in Korea was in 1952. It was the last one during the war. That makes this very last Christmas broadcast from Korea special. As a Minnesota native, whose Minneapolis is considered "the brightest Christmas City in America," I wanted the program to be a winner. Chaplain James C. Moore, also from Minneapolis, suggested I record it at the First Marine Division Chapel. He promised to have a small choir and someone to read a Christmas card home. As I approached the chapel, I could hear the Marines singing. I thought that would be a "grabber," a good way to open the program.

Here is the transcript from the *Marine Corps Show*, broadcast in early January 1953:

SINGING MARINES

One guy didn't think his voice was good enough. "Nonesense," said Chaplain Moore. "Everyone's voice is beautiful singing Christmas carols."

Marines singing Silent Night. (Up full fifteen seconds and under for.)

HILL: (Over choir of Marines.) Many Marines are spending this Christmas in Korea. But despite the thousands of miles separating them from family and friends, the Christmas spirit prevails. For some, it means their very first Christmas away from home. Others will see their very first WHITE Christmas. These men may be miles away from wives, girlfriends, and family, but Christmas is right here with them, just the same. Inside tents and bunkers, pot-bellied stoves are working their magic, while Christmas cards and packages are being eagerly opened by servicemen all over Korea. Nor will the men be without their share of Christmas music that adds so much to the holiday season. Wherever church services are held, men of all creeds are filling the air with familiar carols, like this old favorite, as sung by a group of Marines gathered in the First Marine Division Chapel.

MARINE CHOIR: (Up full for entire song.)

Silent night, holy night
All is calm, all is bright
Round yon Virgin Mother and Child
Holy Infant so tender and mild
Sleep in heavenly peace
Sleep in heavenly peace

Silent night, holy night!
Shepherds quake at the sight
Glories stream from heaven afar
Heavenly hosts sing Alleluia!
Christ, the Savior is born
Christ, the Savior is born

Silent night, holy night
Son of God, love's pure light

Radiant beams from Thy holy face
With the dawn of redeeming grace
Jesus, Lord, at Thy birth
Jesus, Lord at Thy birth.

HILL: Christmas time overseas, just as back in the states, presents a boom in mail. Just ask any Marine over here who has helped with all the extra Christmas cards, letters and packages, and they'll tell you that the men over here are getting their share of mail. And they also sent home an enormous amount of mail telling you folks back home about spending Christmas in Korea. Sgt. Len Pizeznick, of Lackawanna, New York, told his family about spending the holidays over here. He wrote this in his Christmas card:

PIZEZNICK: Hi, folks. I remember listening to the guys back in the states tell me how cold it got around Christmastime here in Korea. Well, it gets chilly, alright, but we're equipped with the finest of cold-weather gear. Back home in Lackawanna, I never did like to wear long underwear. But it sure is a treat to wear it over here. Two days ago your Christmas package arrived. Thanks a lot. Oh, that's right. The guys in my tent wanted to say "Thanks, too." That's one thing about living in a tent. You share. Especially chow. Well, that's about it for now. I hope you have a nice Christmas. We plan to have turkey and all the trimmings. So, Merry Christmas, and I'll see you soon.

Marine choir singing Joy to the World. (Up five seconds and under for.)

HILL: (Over choir.) This is Marine Radio Correspondent Dick Hill, sending you holiday greetings from all the Marines serving in Korea. We return you to the *Marine Corps Show* in Hollywood, California.

TENT RULES

Anyone ever in the military remembers about tent courtesies. You shared your cookies, fruit cake and just about anything else you received in the mail.

We learned that our Christmas Special drew one of the highest radio ratings in the series—a reminder that Christmas sentiment is strong among the public.

Feedback from the program was tremendous. A good reminder that Christmas sentiment packs a powerful wallop with the public. Listeners were especially impressed with the Marine choir. They couldn't believe Marines were that talented when it came to singing. One listener even proposed sending the singing Marines on a tour throughout the United States. (Much like the Iwo Jima Mount Suribachi flag raisers tour, a few years before.) No tour was in the cards for them— or big record contracts—but Chaplain Moore did have them make several appearances among the troops. It turned out to be a "song fest," as the Marines in the audience were encouraged to add their voices. The performances were almost as good as the organized USO shows that performed in Korea.

The program, if broadcast today, might raise a flap among some anti-Christmas groups. Cultural attacks against the celebration of Christmas have multiplied. There is a political-correctness movement to substitute "Happy Holidays" for the traditional "Merry Christmas." As someone who respects all races and religions, I am miffed. Christmas trees and pageants are out of public schools. What is next?

Sands of Iwo Jima, *starring John Wayne, is still a powerful recruiting tool for the Marines. It won a Best Actor Oscar nomination for Wayne in 1949. (Marine Corps Photo)*

24

HOLLYWOOD MARINES

Hollywood has long held the Marine Corps as an American idol. Even before the talkies, filmmakers were cranking out Marine theme movies popular with movie fans. The first to receive full Marine Corps backing was *Star Spangled Banner* in 1917. Since then there have been over 50 made, most with Marine Corps approval. The one I remember best is *Sands of Iwo Jima* with John Wayne. It was 1950 and I went with two of my buddies to see it at the Orpheum Theater in Minneapolis. It had everything you want in a war movie: lots of combat, drama, romance, and laughs. It hooked all three of us. Within two months, my buddies were in the Marines. It took me a little longer. I went in the Marines one year later.

Sands of Iwo Jima is considered the classic Marine Corps film. The John Wayne blockbuster became a powerful enlistment tool for the Marines. Recruiters say it still has plenty of pulling-power even fifty-some years after it was first shown on the big screen. Today, the film draws in eager wannabe Marines to recruiting stations following its late-night television showings. TCM (Turner Classic Movies) appears to rerun it the most.

In 1948, Edmund Grainger, a producer for Republic Pictures, ran across the phrase "sands of Iwo Jima" in a newspaper story and immediately thought of that famous Joe Rosenthal photograph of a group of Marines planting the American flag at the summit of Mount Suribachi. With a title and a climax, he wrote a quick treatment that was later turned into a script by Harry Brown and James Edward Grant. The Marine Corps, knowing John Wayne was signed for the lead, gave permission for full support of the movie. Something unique happened, too: The three Iwo Jima flag-raiser survivors— Navy Corpsman John Bradley, Pfc. Rene Gagnon, and Pfc.

Ira Hayes—play themselves in the movie. (Note: Tony Curtis in 1961 played Ira Hayes in *The Outsider*.)

TOP MOVIES - 1952

High Noon

Singing in the Rain

The Quiet Man

In the summer of 1949, the Republic Pictures team traveled a hundred miles south of Hollywood to Camp Pendleton to make *Sands of Iwo Jima*. On a $1 million budget, Republic made the technically difficult picture. They reenacted two battles—Tarawa and Iwo Jima—and the assault on Mount Suribachi. The technicians built hundreds of plaster palm trees, pillboxes, and gun emplacements, laid thousands of feet of barbed wire, and covered the sand with oil and lampblack to make it look like volcanic ash. The Marines provided troops, Corsair planes from the nearby air base at El Toro, amtracs, cruisers, destroyer escorts, LSTs, and unlimited technical advice.

Wayne played Sgt. John M. Stryker as the quintessential movie Marine. He portrays a hard-nosed sergeant who tries to mold his young recruits into Marines. They hate his unyielding toughness, but he finally wins their respect when he leads them into combat. Wayne was nominated for his first Academy Award for *Sands of Iwo Jima*, and it made him a superstar. The film also featured John Agar (Shirley Temple's first husband), Forrest Tucker, and Adele Mara. It was the largest grossing movie of 1950.

A few years later, Camp Pendleton became "Korea" for the movie, *Retreat, Hell!* This 1952 Hollywood epic showed the Marines' withdrawal from the Chosin Reservoir. The Communist Chinese had just crossed over the Manchurian border and changed the dynamics of the Korean War. A Marine battalion must fight its way out of a frozen mountain pass despite diminishing supplies and ammo. *Retreat, Hell!*, a phrase that relates instantly to military history fans, starred Frank Lovejoy, Richard Carlson, Russ Tamblyn, and Anita Louise.

Three years later came the most popular Marine movie ever, based on box-office receipts, titled *Battle Cry*. It was written by a former Marine, Leon Uris, and was directed by Raoul Walsh. The film was a fictional account of World War II. It touched on combat situations and the lighter side of life in the Marine Corps in off-duty hours. It starred Van Heflin, Aldo Ray, and James Whitmore. Supporting players included Mona Freeman, Raymond Massey, and Tab Hunter. *Battle Cry* also received the Marine Corps' backing.

Good news for movie buffs: I've compiled a list of every Hollywood film—from the silent era to 2005—with a Marine theme. During World War II and the Korean conflict, film producers were the busiest: they made 19 features. In my mind, the films made in the 1940's and 1950s were some the best: *Wake Island, Guadalcanal Diary, Gung Ho, Sands of Iwo Jima*, and *Battle Cry*. And one, a comedy, *Hail the Conquering Hero*.

Review the list carefully. Then check to see how many of the 50-plus films you've seen. If it's over 35, you beat me.

MARINE MOVIES

Pre-1930s

Star Spangled Banner
The Unbeliever

MOVIE JUNKIE

I admit it. I love movies. Especially pictures with a Marine Corps theme. Check the below roster of Marine movies to see how many you've seen.

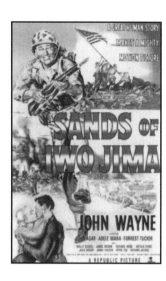

A poster of the John Wayne epic, Sands of Iwo Jima. *Marine recruiters say the fillm still has drawing power for recruits. (Marine Corps Photo)*

1960s

Hell to Eternity
All the Young Men
The Outsider
Marines, Let's Go
Gomer Pyle, U.S.M.C.
Ambush Bay

1970s

Baa Baa, Black Sheep (TV)
Tribes (TV)
The Wind and the Lion
Boys in Company C
MacArthur

1980s

Anybody's Son Will do
Heartbreak Ridge
Full Metal Jacket
Death Before Dishonor
Major Dad
Born on the Fourth of July
The Siege on Firebase Gloria

1990s

A Few Good Men
Major Payne
The Walking Dead
Xtro: Watch the Skies
Most Wanted

LIGHTS! ACTION!

Hollywood is neat duty. Two of my PIO buddies, Bob Fugate and Joe Hensley, pulled it after Korea.

2000s

Green Dragon
Windtalkers
Wake Island: Alamo of the Pacific (TV)
The Code Talkers: A Secret Code of Honor
Stateside
Flags of Our Fathers

CALL OF DUTY

John Wayne's Sands of Iwo Jima, *still pulls recruits into the Marines.*

The above pictures represent a lot of history, action, drama, romance, laughs, and memories for lots of us. Many are now on DVD so you can re-screen your favorites, or see those films you missed. I missed *Windtalkers* and intend to get the DVD. If you like laughs, pick up a copy of *Hail the Conquering Hero*. This 1944 Preston Sturges movie, starring Eddie Bracken and Ella Raines, is a classic. Having been discharged from the Marines for hayfever, Woodrow Pershing Truesmith (Eddie Bracken) delays the return to his hometown, feeling he's a failure. He meets up with a group of Marines who befriend him and encourage him to return home to his widowed mother. They fabricate a story that he was wounded in battle with an honorable discharge. He wears a uniform complete with medals and gets a hero's welcome that he does not want. Great supporting cast: William Demarest, Raymond Walburn, and Franklin Pangborn.

Many Hollywood workers and personalities joined the Marines when they were needed. Here are some:

REAL HOLLYWOOD MARINES

Don Adams

Nick Adams

MacDonald Carey

Brian Dennehy

Glenn Ford

James Franciscus

Christopher George

Gene Hackman

Sterling Hayden

Louis Hayward

Harvey Keitel

Brian Keith

Bill Lundigan

George Maharis

Jock Mahoney

Lee Marvin

Tim Matheson

Steve McQueen

Hugh O'Brien

George Peppard

Tyrone Power

Burt Reynolds

Robert Ryan

John Russell

George C. Scott

Bo Svenson

Robert Wagner

James Whitmore

Jonathan Winters

Other notables in the entertainment field that served in the Marine Corps:

RADIO AND TELEVISION PERSONALITIES

Bea Arthur

Drew Carey

Hodding Carter

Mike Connors

Don Imus

Keith Jackson

Bob Keeshan

Ed McMahon

Martin Milner

Oliver North

Mark Russell

Bernard Shaw

Larry Wilcox

Montel Williams

The author, second from left, is decorated for his Korean War service. Ceremony was at the El Toro Marine Corps Air Station, California, July 1953. (Marine Corps Photo)

25

ESPRIT DE CORPS

Before battle, everyone wonders how they will measure up. No one wants to let his buddy down. I quickly learned on the line in Korea that there is strength in numbers. I was on an assignment to tape-record several men from the First Platoon, "Able" Company, Seventh Marine Regiment. First, their platoon handled a recon mission, and I was invited to tag along. The mission was to chart the Chinese position, identify their artillery location and secure the enemy's troop strength. Some new replacements felt a little queasy, as I did. This was my maiden venture beyond the MLR into no-man's-land. The veterans quickly saw our concern. We were patted on the back and told, "Don't worry." It came to me. And it was all so simple. The strong supported the weak to strengthen the group's potential for success. In psychological terms, the leaders encouraged or motivated the followers by setting an example. I was seeing *esprit de corps* in action: *"The spirit of comradeship, enthusiasm and devotion to a common cause among the members of group."* In simpler terms, *"the spirit of a group."* Our platoon leader, a 2nd lieutenant, explained to me what was happening: "We've got to work together. Or it won't work." For whatever reason, no other military service has been able to execute this group-spirit concept with such consistency as the U.S. Marine Corps.

My brother, Kenny, likes to downplay the notion that there is a mystique about the Marine Corps. You have to know Kenny. He was in the army in WW II and I was the Marine in the family from the Korean War. He keeps reminding me that his war was the one that counted. After a second-helping backyard barbecue at my place, we were lounging in the lawn chairs with a cool one. Our wives were inside, probably watching Liberace on television.

The author, right, with John Chalk, Leatherneck *magazine artist, March 1953. Both were young, eager and gung ho. (Author's Collection)*

He made the first move. "You Marines think you're invincible. Like Superman or Spider-Man. That's a bunch of crock," he jealously said.

It was time to challenge him. That's when I reached in my pocket and showed him a small, tattered note pad. On the cover it read: *Pvt. R. N. Hill, November 1951.* "Do you still have your notes from basic training, Kenny?" I asked, kind of knowing he probably never took notes during basic training. That is the kind of guy he was. It is a wonder we won the war.

"Jesus!" he said. He could not believe his eyes when he scanned my note pad. "This is from your boot camp days? Wow, this had gotta be—what—50 years ago. You took all these notes?"

"Sure. School was a big part of boot camp. Take a look under Marine traditions."

He flipped a few pages than stopped. "Here it is. Here's something you scribbled. Looks like a French word—*esprit de corps*?"

"I remember the day we discussed it," I recalled. "*Esprit de corps*. It's the fuel that drives the Marine Corps. Does it give the definition?" I asked.

He nodded yes.

"See if I remember it. Esprit de corps: *It's the spirit of comradeship, enthusiasm and devotion to a common cause among the members of a group.*"

"Jesus. How could you remember that?" he halfway complimented me.

"Kenny, didn't you use *esprit de corps* in the Army?" I probed.

"Hell no," he fired back. "The Army didn't need it. We were pretty damn well organized without it. And we didn't use that gung ho shit, either."

My, my! My older brother's shorts must be in a bind. That, or he is a little jealous of the Marine Corps— again. I decided to keep peace in the family and shift subjects. We had enough battle talk for one night. Kenny, my own brother, would not understand the value of group spirit, anyway. And in fairness to him, lots of people—and companies, for that matter—did not.

One that did was Campbell Mithun, an advertising agency I joined after leaving the Marines. It was most famous for its Hamms Beer "Sky Blue Waters" television commercials. The campaign was the envy of the industry and still remembered by many consumers and studied in marketing classes. The campaign featured a refreshing lake country setting, musical tom-toms, and a lovable bear. (The bear was one of the first animated icons in television). I wish I could say I developed the idea. But it took a former Walt Disney artist, Cleo Hovel, to come up with the concept. I was involved in many of the test commercials. My Marine Radio Correspondent days gave me the experience for many "voice over" commercials at the agency's Chicago office.

I wasn't there a month when I noticed the strong similarity between Ray Mithun, president, and the Marine Corps. For starters, both were pioneers and innovators. Each liked to cut new patterns and set

My very own brother liked to put down the Marine Corps. He argued that the Army was superior to the Marines. And he sure got mad when he could never win the debate.

After service I went with an ad agency in Minneapolis. Campbell Mithun was good but wanted to be better. Ray Mithun, president, turned to the Marines for more productivity.

the pace. Both were taskmasters and leaders in their respective fields. In the agency's thirtieth year, other "hotter" shops were growing faster than CM. (In the ad biz, status quo is unacceptable.) One problem: Campbell Mithun's headquarters was in Minneapolis. Many blue-chip prospects mistakenly thought great advertising could only come from out east. The agency was soon to turn this "Dark Ages" mentality around. Ray Mithun first needed to pump up his people with Marine Corps style "group spirit." Perhaps we just needed a "kick in the pants" or some new direction.

Here, in summary, are his opening remarks to the 100 of us at the Chicago O'Hare Inn on June 17, 1966:

> I have some concerns. I called this meeting for just one reason: To talk...talk...talk. To talk about our creative activity—and our creative *philosophy*. Until everyone in this room understands the creative *attitude* we want to prevail in this agency. In so doing, we will talk about our creative spirit, our creative philosophy and our methods. And right from the beginning I want you to know that I am most anxious for the right *esprit de corps* in this organization. And those of you with Marine Corps roots will know what I'm talking about.

I liked what I was hearing from our leader. A few of my colleagues glanced at me, knowing I was a former Marine. The room was quiet, unlike most seminars that I had attended. His message was getting across. Then he used a smart ploy of an effective speaker. He paused for what seemed like forever. We were on the edges of our chairs. Then he continued:

"When a whole group of people act with the same spirit, it becomes what the Marine Corps calls *esprit de corps*. A French word, the dictionary says."

Then he stopped and did the unexpected. Well known for sharing the stage with his people, he called on Gene Peterson. A short, studious, bald man in his fifties, Gene was the most respected copywriter in the agency. As he came up to the stage, Ray Mithun handed him what had to be the largest Webster dictionary ever made:

> Gene. You can see better than I can. Please give us the Webster meaning of *esprit de corps*.

Ray Mithun, co-founder of Campbell Mithun and the author's former boss. Mithun took a page from the Marines and instilled more group spirit among his people. (Photo Courtesy Campbell Mithun)

A smart tactic. The words would not be coming from Mithun, now. Someone else was going to deliver them. It was obviously unrehearsed, which only added excitement to the meeting. Mithun could not have picked a better presenter. Peterson was calm. Took his time. Even adjusted the microphone to his liking. Then, in a rich, beautiful voice, he slowly played his part:

> *Esprit de Corps*—a common spirit of comradeship, enthusiasm and devotion to a cause among the members of a group.

The rest of Mr. Mithun's presentation was simple and direct. He begged for action. Besides a new group spirit to help drive the agency, he called for "new track" to lead the agency to a leadership position. He wanted us all to be "trailblazers." His people, including me, responded enthusiastically. In an industry that increasingly seems to know only winners and losers, Campbell Mithun, like the Marines, has emerged a winner. Founded and still firmly based in Minneapolis, this growing, creative coast-to-coast agency stays

GROUP SPIRIT

Nobody knows esprit de corps *like the Marine Corps*

true to Mr. Mithun's vision and pioneering concept. (Raymond O. Mithun died in 1998.) National advertisers that might have turned to New York have discovered "selling power" with CM in Minneapolis. Ranked as the 21st largest agency in the United States, its clients include Verizon Wireless, Burger King, H&R Block, General Mills, Andersen Windows, Land O' Lakes, and Toro Mowers. I was proud to have worked for Ray Mithun, an advertising legend and a member of the Advertising Hall of Fame, the industry's most prestigious honor.

Esprit de corps is the fuel that drives the Marines and other organizations. Smart CEOs know that besides financial resources, it takes individuals to back an organization's basic philosophy, spirit, and drive. Wal-Mart is an excellent example. Sam Walton, the founder, tapped his people's energy and developed a teampower that is the envy of the industry. From out of nowhere they became the nation's number one retailer. As the company grew it rolled over two sleeping giants, Sears and K-Mart. Wal-Mart surprised Wall Street, also. Today they are first on the Fortune 500, a reminder that people with one common goal can be a driving force to help their organization stand out. Something that I tell young people starting their career: *"Use all of the innovation, energy, and creativity at your command to help reduce costs and serve your company better. And above all, be a team person."* (NFL coaches have been known to trade players with outstanding individual skills that refuse to be a team player.)

Enjoy Top 20 Lists like I do? See how many of your favorite companies make the cut. The connection? All are good examples of organizations using camaraderie to pursue excellence. Check out the latest *crème de la crème*:

Dick Hill's ESPRIT DE CORPS 20
Examples of Outstanding Group Spirit

1. U.S. Marine Corps* – Quantico, Virginia
2. Wal-Mart – Bentonville, Arkansas
3. Apple Computer – Cupertino, California
4. McDonald's – Oak Brook, Illinois
5. Nordstrom – Seattle, Washington
6. General Mills – Minneapolis, Minnesota
7. Fox News – New York city, New York
8. Proctor & Gamble – Cincinnati, Ohio
9. Walt Disney – Burbank, California
10. Campbell Mithun Advertising* – Minneapolis, Minnesota
11. Southwest Airlines – Dallas, Texas
12. MGM Mirage – Las Vegas, Nevada
13. Barnes & Noble – New York city, New York
14. The Minnesota State Fair – Saint Paul, Minnesota
15. UPS – Atlanta, Georgia
16. Target – Minneapolis, Minnesota
17. FedEx Kinko's – Memphis, Tennessee
18. Starbucks Coffee – Seattle, Washington
19. Best Buy – Richfield, Minnesota
20. Saturn Automobile – Spring Hill, Tennessee

Organizations the author has served

SECRET FOR SUCCESS

Besides financial resources, it takes individuals to back an organization's basic philosophy, spirit and drive.

An early classic enlistment poster that inspired many young people to join the Marines. (Marine Corps Photo)

26

THE FEW, THE PROUD

Most kids like to dream. I know I did. While attending Phillips Junior High School in Minneapolis, I could see myself strutting around in Marine dress blues. It was the coolest uniform in all the armed forces. I had first seen sharp-looking Marine guards wearing their "blues" on recruiting posters. With that bright red stripe running down the side of the trousers. Cool! To wear them, I found out, you must earn them first. I did. I got my dress blues. And a whole lot more. I belonged to the best military group anywhere—The Few and the Proud. After studying the Marine Corps traditions and legends in boot camp—discipline, courage, *esprit de corps*, and such—I was impressed with the Marine Corps' history and military performance. After leaving service, the lessons learned helped shape my life and business career. The real-life experiences from the Marines stay with you: being competitive, successful, organized, focused, motivated, and a team player. According to friends, the Marines made me a "can-do" guy.

Always ahead of the curve, the U.S. Marine Corps was using niche marketing long before the term was invented. Many Fortune 500 companies would love to have a brand image as memorable as the Marines. Proctor & Gamble and 3M, leaders in their fields, would respect the Marines' market position as the leading "brand" in its industry. The Marine mystique is a marketing marvel. Much of the credit goes to the Marine Public Affairs people. They operate the most powerful PR machine in the military—some say the most powerful in the world. The press coverage they have landed is the front-page variety that is a benchmark in the PR field. Their advertising message: *The Few. The Proud. The Marines* instantly connects with the public. It has the best recall of any recruiting theme or slogan in the marketplace. Marines also own one of America's most famous icons from

MISTY MARINES

There isn't a Marine living that doesn't wipe his eyes after viewing the Iwo Jima War Monument.

World War II: the Iwo Jima War Monument near the Arlington National Cemetery in Virginia. Seen it? The image of five Marines and a Navy corpsman raising an American flag atop Mount Suribachi during World War II is well known to most Americans from photos and films. Seen in person, the bronze 78-foot statue stirs emotions. The memorial is dedicated to all U.S. Marines who died in battle. I saw a small model of it before construction. Even that tiny replica made my eyes misty.

During the static period of the Korean War from 1952–1953, the United Nations' military leaders knew what they were doing when they positioned the First Marine Division toe-to-toe with the Chinese Communist Army on the MLR. The ever-ready Marines were the best match for this tough enemy, more so than the U.S. Army or the fifteen other UN forces. Most units faced the North Korean Peoples Army, because the North Korean soldiers had less battlefield training and equipment than their counterparts did. As one young platoon leader told me during a radio interview: *"I fought both the Chinese and the North Koreans. I could barely tell them apart. But the Chinese hated us worst."*

At an American Legion dinner after the Korean War, I heard this same subject discussed. A former soldier and former Marine, who both fought in Korea, were rehashing the war. The Leatherneck reminded his friend that the Eighth Army had lighter duty by facing the North Korean People's Army. The Corps, on the other hand, he reminded the soldier, took on the Communist Chinese Army. The dogface, a little perturbed at the remark, and defending his position, got the last word by saying: "Oh, I suppose the North Koreans were only using stun guns out there. Those sure looked like real bullets that flew by me." Then furthering the point, he lifted his left trouser to reveal a nasty-looking scar in his leg.

"Good God!" the Marine reacted to both the wound and his embarrassment. He realized his *faux pas*. Recovering from his big blunder he blurted out: "Shrapnel?"

The soldier, letting his trouser leg down, said: "Well, at least you know something about war wounds. Yeah! Shrapnel from one of their lousy grenades."

I was happy to see the two spend the next hour or so deep into the Korean War, and the Marine with new respect for the U.S. Army. The soldier, I noticed, did not have to buy another Budweiser that night.

Not all of *the few and the proud* are regulars. Marine reserves played an important part in Korea. One key job in public affairs went to reservist Capt. Bem Price. A reporter for Associated Press, he covered the early days of the Korean War. Then the Marines activated him. After some catch-up training stateside, he was sent back to Korea where he was Public Information Officer of the First Marine Division's PIO section (now Public Affairs). Besides working closely with the civilian press, he oversaw the Combat Correspondents, including writers, photographers, and radio correspondents. Quite often after previewing my radio tapes he had them transcribed and made into press releases for the media to use for newspaper publication and for radio broadcast.

TOUGHEST ENEMY?

Not every argument between a soldier and a Marine ends in agreement. This one did. They both conceded that the North Koreans were just as tough as the Red Chinese.

Probably the most famous reservist—maybe in all the military—was Ted Williams. The Boston Red Sox slugger was a jet fighter pilot with the First Marine Air Wing. He had the world media after him for stories. I was lucky to be at the right place at the right time and scored an interview with him on the USS *Haven*, a hospital ship, in April 1953. After Korea, Williams was awarded an Air Medal, two Gold Stars, and a medical discharge. He was discharged from reserve status, too.

No one collected war memorabilia like my buddies did in Korea. They stashed their bounty everywhere. Under bunks, in duffel bags and shave kits, on walls, and, if small enough, in their pockets. I am talking about enemy flags, swords, bugles, knives, pistols, burp guns, rifles, bullets, helmets, pieces of uniforms, jewelry, documents, and photos. It was obvious they wanted a piece of the war to take home with them.

Those same Marines are known to boast a bit about their beloved Corps. And why not? Marines have lots to bust their buttons about:

30 REASONS TO LOVE THE MARINE CORPS

1. **Classiest uniform** – Dress Blues (The red stripe represents the blood shed in battle.)
2. **Best slogans** – "Send in the Marines." "Tell it to the Marines." "First to fight."
3. **Best recruiting theme** – "The Few. The Proud. The Marines."
4. **Neatest logo** – The Marine eagle, globe and anchor. (Representing air, land and sea)
5. **Best nickname** – Leathernecks

6. **Toughest basic training** – Marine boot camp
7. **Best instructors** – Marine DIs (Drill Instructors)
8. **Most beautiful recruit depot** – Marine Corps Recruit Depot, San Diego, California
9. **Best military song** – The Marine Hymn (This is the only service song officially sanctioned by Congress.)
10. **Image** – Recognized as the "#1 brand" in the military.
11. **Corpsmen** – Battlefield Marines get medical aid from U.S. Navy Corpsmen. God bless 'em.
12. **Status** – Sailors live and work on ships. Marines go on cruises; then hit the shore.
13. **Toughest mascot** – Marines have the bulldog; the Navy has got a goat.
14. **Best haircut** – You cannot have a bad hair day with a Marine high and tight.
15. **Best personalized license plate** – "1775." It is the Marine Commandant's vehicle.
16. **First in orbit** – Marine fighter pilot, John Glenn. (Ted Williams' CO in Korea)
17. **Best war movie** – *Sands of Iwo Jima* starring John Wayne.
18. **Tax dollar value** – Marines do it all for less. Just six cents of every dollar spent on defense goes to the Marine Corps.
19. **Self-sufficient divisions** – Each a small army. It carries its own ground force, air force, artillery, tank, supply, medical, engineering and other support battalions and companies.
20. **Best motto** – Semper Fidelis; always faithful.

November 10 is a red-letter day for every Leatherneck—*past and present. It is the Marine Corps birthday and celebrated throughout the world.*

21. **Memorable battles** – Iwo Jima, Guadalcanal, Wake Island, Guam, Peleliu, Tarawa, Inchon landing, Chosin Reservoir, and more.

22. **Greatest legend** – Lt. General Lewis B. "Chesty" Puller

23. **Hollywood Marines** – Glenn Ford, Gene Hackman, Sterling Hayden, Lee Marvin, Steve McQueen, Tyrone Power, Burt Reynolds, George C. Scott, and many more

24. **Best World War II Memorial** – Iwo Jima flag-raising statue, Arlington, Virginia.

25. **Unity** – Every Marine is a rifleman.

26. **Top Guns – Marine snipers**. – One shot, one kill, one thousand yards.

26. **Marine sports icon** – Capt. Ted Williams (served in World War II & Korea)

27. **Marines take care of their own** – Nobody's left behind on the battlefield, dead or alive.

28. **Most famous saying** – *"Retreat, Hell!"* By General Oliver P. Smith, Commander, First Marine Division, Korea, Dec. 1950. *"Retreat, Hell! We're just attacking in another direction."*

29. **Esprit de corps** – It is what makes the Marines special. *"The spirit of a group; enthusiasm and devotion to the cause among the members of an organization."*

30. **Biggest birthday bash** – The Founding Fathers established the U.S. Marine Corps on November, 10, 1775. Celebrated at every Marine post and time zone in the world.

GLOSSARY

Slang: The military, like all large, exclusive organizations, develops slang—buzz words—as a means of identification. Military slang or lingo is also used to reinforce the inter-service rivalries. Some of the terms have been considered derogatory to varying degrees and attempts have been made to eliminate them. But so far, to no avail.

Bad paper – Dishonorable discharge

Blow away – Kill

Bouncy Betty – Land mine

Bug Juice – Sweetened water or drink

Buy the farm – To die

Flak jacket – Armored vest

Friendlies – South Koreans

Goof off – Kill time

Gooks – Chinese and Koreans

Goose it – Step on it

Gung ho – Ready, fired up, driven

Hash marks – Service stripes on the sleeve; one stripe = 4 yrs

Head – Latrine or bathroom

Honey bucket detail – Men assigned to emptying buckets of latrine sewage

Jarhead – What sailors call Marines

Lock and load – An informal command to prepare to fight

Mama-san & Papa-san – Korean adults

Number one – The best

Number ten – The worst

Over the hump – Halfway through your enlistment

PX – Post exchange; store on base

PT – Physical training

Pimple – Small hill

Put that in your mess kit – Final word

Red Tide – Masses of Communist Chinese

Saddle-up – Get ready for next objective

Screwed, blued and tattooed – Cheated

Square away – Clean up

Wet roadblock – The Yalu River. UN forces forbidden to cross in pursuit of enemy

Abbreviations

A/1/7 – Able Company, 1st Battalion, 7th Regiment

AFRS – Armed Forces Radio Service

AP – Associated Press

BAR – Browning Automatic Rifle

BN – Battalion

CC – Combat Correspondent

CMC – Commandant of the Marine Corps

CO – Commanding officer

CP – Command post; Combat Photographer

COP – Command Outpost (Berlin, East Berlin, Carson, Elko, Reno and Vegas)

DI – Drill instructor

DivHQ – Division headquarters

DPA, DivPA – Division of Public Affairs

DPI – Division of Public Information

FMFPac – Fleet Marine Force, Pacific

G-1 – Personnel

G-2 – Intelligence

G-3 – Operations

G-4 – Supply

H&S – Headquarters and Service

HQ – Headquarters

HQMC – Headquarters, Marine Corps

INS – International News Service

KIA – Killed in Action

KMC – Korean Marine Corps

LST – Landing ship tank

MASH – Mobile Army Surgical Hospital

MCB – Marine Corps Base

MEB – Marine expeditionary brigade

MIA – Missing in Action

MLR – Main Line of Resistance

MP – Military Police

MOS – Military occupational specialty

NCOIC – Noncommissioned officer-in-charge

Noncom – Noncommissioned officer

OIC – Officer in charge

OPLR – Outpost Line of Resistance

OSS – Office of Strategic Services

PA – Public Affairs

PAO – Public Affairs office or officer

PIO – Public Information Office, Public Information
officer

POW – Prisoner of War

PR – Public relations

PRO – Public relations officer

PX – Post exchange

Recon – Reconnaissance

ROK – Republic of Korea

S&S – *Stars and Stripes* newspaper

SOP – Standard Operating Procedures

SP – Shore Patrol

TAD – Temporary Additional Duty

TO&E – Table of Organization & Equipment

UP – United Press

USA – United States Army

USAF – United States Air Force

USCG – United States Coast Guard

USFJ – U.S. Forces, Japan

USMC – United States Marine Corps

USMCCCA – United States Marine Corps Combat
   Correspondents Association

USMCR – United States Marine Corps Reserve

USN – United States Navy

WIA – Wounded in Action

WWI – World War One

WWII – World War Two

Marine Ranks: Enlisted Personnel

Pvt. – Private

Pfc. – Private First Class

LCpl. – Lance Corporal

Cpl. – Corporal

Sgt. – Sergeant

SSgt. – Staff Sergeant

GySgt. – Gunnery Sergeant

MSgt. – Master Sergeant

SgtMaj. – Sergeant Major

MGySgt. – Master Gunnery Sergeant

Marine Ranks: Commissioned Officers

2nd Lt. – Second Lieutenant

lst Lt. – First Lieutenant

Capt. – Captain

Maj. – Major

Lt. Col. – Lieutenant Colonel

Col. – Colonel

Brig. Gen. – Brigadier General

Maj. Gen. – Major General

Lt. Gen. – Lieutenant General

Gen. – General; Commandant of the Marine Corps

ABOUT THE AUTHOR

Dick Hill was born to be a Marine Correspondent. As a kid he practiced his trade by talking into a kitchen spoon. While attending college, he interned at WCCO, a leading radio station in Minneapolis. There he learned broadcasting inside-out during the Golden Age of Radio. When only 18, he read the midnight news on the giant 50,000-watt station. Hill is a graduate of the University of Minnesota. He had a 35-year-career in advertising. For 12 of those years he worked for Campbell Mithun in Chicago, one of the top ad agencies. After retirement he put his expertise into a book for small business: *Advertising That Sells*. He still dabbles in advertising. He is also a military history buff, e-mail enthusiast, and proud member of the United States Marine Corps Combat Correspondents Association. He lives in Edina, Minnesota, with his wife, Mary.